GOD'S ANSWERS

FOR YOUR TIMES OF TROUBLE

DAVID CERULLO

INSPIRATION
MINISTRIES

GOD'S ANSWERS
for Your Times of Trouble

David Cerullo

Copyright © 2005, 2011 by David Cerullo
ISBN 978-1-887600-73-6
All Scripture quotations, unless otherwise indicated,
are from the New American Standard Bible, © copyright 1960, 1962,
1963, 1968, 1971, 1972, 1973, 1975, 1977, 1995 by the Lockman
Foundation. Used by permission.

Scriptures marked KJV are taken from the
Holy Bible, King James Version.

Published by
INSPIRATION MINISTRIES
P.O. Box 7750
Charlotte, NC 28241
inspiration.org

Printed in the United States of America.

DEDICATION

THIS BOOK IS DEDICATED to all those who are enduring times of trouble. God has promised to never leave you or forsake you.

Through every moment of every day, He is right by your side, taking you by the hand, and He will see you through. May you understand that God loves you *unconditionally.* He has a wonderful plan for your life, and through Him, you can be more than a conqueror in every troubled moment that you face.

As you endeavor to overcome the challenges of life, may this book help to guide you through the Word of God to a position of empowerment and a place of permanent peace.

God Bless You!

David

CONTENTS

Introduction

INTRODUCTION

AT MANY JUNCTURES OF LIFE you will face troubled times...times when you are concerned about some upcoming event...times when you are uneasy, apprehensive, or even fearful.

Perhaps you've just received a bad report from your doctor...or you have lost your job. It may be that a mountain of bills and financial obligations are crashing down and you can't see any hope for escape.

Perhaps your son or daughter is running with the wrong crowd or is using drugs...or your spouse has been unfaithful and your marriage is in trouble.

THE FATHER'S PEACE

Regardless of what you are facing or the cause of your anxiety, remember these words from Scripture: *"Be anxious for nothing, but in everything by prayer and supplication, with thanksgiving, let your requests be made known to God. And the peace of God, which surpasses all comprehension, will guard your hearts and your minds in Christ Jesus"* (Philippians 4:6-7).

I want you to know that as a Christian, you can be surrounded by the Father's joy, peace, and protection—despite what is swirling in the world around you.

The answers you will find in this book are not mine. They are based on God's Word—the first place we must turn in a time of crisis. It is here where you will receive the necessary wisdom, strength, and comfort.

We want you to know that God loves you, and you never need to doubt His concern for your well-being. When your faith needs strengthening—when you need courage—when you need wisdom to know what to do—draw on His Word for blessing and encouragement.

"WHERE DO I TURN?"

As you will learn, it's important to lean on God's truth and rest in His arms of love and compassion. This is where you will find Divine help and guidance.

Scripture reminds us to *"Trust in the Lord with all your heart, and do not lean on your own understanding. In all your ways acknowledge Him, and He will make your paths straight"* (Proverbs 3:5-6).

In troubled times, we are often tempted to rely on family, friends, associates, or those in the world for assurance. Instead, we must turn to God's unchanging Word and let His peace flood our hearts and minds. This will guard us from Satan's attempts to bring fear or destruction into our lives.

KEYS TO MIRACLES

I encourage you to allow the Holy Spirit to supernaturally deposit the Word into your mind, soul, and spirit. Allow the Scriptures I have included in this book to soak into your very being. They will guide your life, give you strength and stability, and reveal steps to take when you feel discouraged, lonely, or confused.

Hidden within His Word are keys to miracles—enough to meet every crisis you will ever face.

You will find, as did the psalmist David, *"Thy Word is a lamp unto my feet and a light unto my path"* (Psalm 119:105 KJV).

MY PRAYER FOR YOU

This book is not a psychology text or a medical reference. It is a Biblical response to the epidemic of fear, worry, and anxiety infecting our world. What you are about to read is in complete harmony with God's established Truth.

I love you and pray that this message will fortify and comfort you through your troubled times. I pray that it will help to guide you in facing life's difficulties and show you how to defeat every attempt of the devil, the enemy of your soul.

– *David Cerullo*

CHAPTER ONE

Why Are We Troubled?

I AM THRILLED that you are reading this book. Why? Because I am concerned about you and want you to understand that, regardless of the obstacles you face, there is help and there is hope.

We have traveled through space, built great cities, obtained vast knowledge, and today we enjoy conveniences beyond our wildest dreams—yet we are troubled. Fear and apprehension have invaded our lives like an invisible virus.

You can talk to an executive on Wall Street or a housewife in Wisconsin and sense uneasiness, even worry, about their circumstances:

- "I'm concerned about the friends my children are hanging out with."
- "The doctor tells me not to be alarmed, but I've heard of people who have died from my condition."
- "I'm fearful about the economy. What will happen to my retirement fund?"

Others are anxious about relationships—jealousy, a bitter argument, a broken marriage. Is it any wonder that the pharmaceutical industry reaps billions of dollars from medications designed to ease our anxiety and relieve our stress?

- Children are rebelling against parents.
- Neighbors are battling neighbors.
- The Body of Christ is experiencing strife.
- Families are being torn apart.

We are also apprehensive about our physical safety—installing extra locks and high-tech alarm systems. Like Hezekiah, we wonder, *"Is it not good, if peace and truth be in my days?"* (2 Kings 20:19 KJV).

DON'T FEEL ALONE

Psychologists inform us that one in every eight Americans between the ages of 18 and 54 suffers from an anxiety disorder. That's nearly 20 million people!

What we are experiencing is not just external stress; we are struggling with an internal reaction to circumstance we can't control.

Anxiety, the twin of worry, can affect much more than your mind. It can increase blood pressure, cause rapid heartbeat, and result in physical reactions from feeling faint to a full-fledged panic attack. As Job expresses it, *"I am seething within and cannot relax; days of affliction confront me"* (Job 30:27).

You may wonder, "If the Lord is the Prince of Peace

and I am His child, why is my life so consumed with worry and tension?" It's a valid question—and one we will address.

When life comes crashing down, don't feel alone. The greatest heroes of faith had their moments of heartbreak and despair. More than once, David cried out, *"My God, my God, why have You forsaken me? Far from my deliverance are the words of my groaning"* (Psalm 22:1).

Continue reading the next few verses and you'll find a man who feels abandoned and helpless. He complains that he is being...

- Ignored (v.2)
- Despised and rejected (v.6)
- Ridiculed for his faith (v.7)
- Taunted by vicious enemies (v. 12)
- Drained and on the verge of death (v.15)
- Surrounded by a murderous mob (v.16)

Perhaps you have felt burdened with similar feelings—and have cried yourself to sleep. Like David, you have said, *"I am weary with my sighing; every night I make my bed swim, I dissolve my couch with my tears. My eye has wasted away with grief; it has become old because of all my adversaries"* (Psalm 6:6-7).

Let me assure you that just because you *"walk through the valley of the shadow of death"* (Psalm 23:4), it does not mean that God has forgotten you. As we will discover, there is an escape route from despair.

My friend, Jesus knows exactly what you are going

through—He's been there. He understands and even feels your pain and suffering because of what He endured on the Cross. As the writer of Hebrews states, *"For we do not have a high priest who cannot sympathize with our weaknesses, but One who has been tempted in all things as we are, yet without sin"* (Hebrews 4:15).

ROUGH TREATMENT

Life isn't always clear skies and smooth seas—you will have troubled times.

The apostles were *"as men condemned to death; because we have become a spectacle to the world, both to angels and to men. We are fools for Christ's sake....To this present hour we are both hungry and thirsty, and are poorly clothed, and are roughly treated, and are homeless; and we toil, working with our own hands; when we are reviled, we bless; when we are persecuted, we endure; when we are slandered, we try to conciliate; we have become as the scum of the world, the dregs of all things, even until now"* (1 Corinthians 4:9-13).

Many people believe that being a Christian protects them from hardship. The Blood of Jesus does cover us, but we do not get a "free pass" from troubles. Even Believers experience difficulties.

STONED AND SHIPWRECKED

If you want to meet a man whose life was filled with troubled times, examine the autobiography of the Apostle Paul—the missionary/evangelist who wrote two-thirds of the New Testament.

Comparing himself with others, he asks, *"Are they Hebrews? So am I. Are they Israelites? So am I. Are they descendants of Abraham? So am I. Are they servants of Christ?—I speak as if insane—I more so; in far more labors, in far more imprisonments, beaten times without number, often in danger of death"* (2 Corinthians 11: 22-23).

Then Paul gives the specifics of his suffering for the cause of Christ. *"Five times I received from the Jews thirty-nine lashes. Three times I was beaten with rods, once I was stoned, three times I was shipwrecked, a night and a day I have spent in the deep. I have been on frequent journeys, in dangers from rivers, dangers from robbers, dangers from my countrymen, dangers from the Gentiles, dangers in the city, dangers in the wilderness, dangers on the sea, dangers among false brethren; I have been in labor and hardship, through many sleepless nights, in hunger and thirst, often without food, in cold and exposure. Apart from such external things, there is the daily pressure on me of concern for all the churches"* (vs. 24-28).

AGONIZING HARDSHIPS

Does that chronicle reflect a life filled with material comforts and possessions? The Apostle wasn't staying at the presidential suite in the Ritz Carlton and chauffeur-driven to his meetings in a stretch limo flanked by security guards! Here was a man who had witnessed mighty miracles and felt the wonder-working power of God in his life, yet he still experienced agonizing hardships.

Given what Paul went through, the average Joe today would say, "Enough already! I quit!"

I want you to take comfort in the fact that, regardless of the attacks, the Lord "shall cover thee with His feathers, and under His wings shalt thou trust: His truth shall be thy shield and buckler" (Psalm 91:4 KJV).

Take a moment to realize that you are surrounded by heavenly protection: *"For He will give His angels charge concerning you, to guard you in all your ways. They will bear you up in their hands, that you do not strike your foot against a stone"* (Psalm 91:11-12).

A CRISIS IN CANADA

No one is immune to dark clouds and deep valleys. We all walk through them. The Word declares, "Through many tribulations we must enter the kingdom of God" *(Acts 14:22).*

I was invited to minister at a church in the beautiful city of Montreal, Canada, and my wife Barbara accompanied me on the trip.

That Sunday morning, there was a great move of the Holy Spirit in the service, and it was evident that peoples' hearts were challenged.

Later that day, during a meal the pastor had arranged for us, I began feeling discomfort in my stomach, but had no idea what could be the cause. Trying to self-diagnose, I thought, "Oh, I've probably eaten something that doesn't agree with me."

Over the next few hours, the pain intensified, and Barbara became quite concerned.

BEYOND PAIN

It was nearly 6:00 p.m., and I had somehow mustered enough energy to make my way to the pastor's study, ready for the evening service. By this time, I was in complete agony with severe pain in the lower right quadrant of my body.

My family can attest to the fact that I am not the kind of person who relishes a trip to the doctor—not that I have anything against them. I have a high tolerance for pain, yet this was beyond anything I had ever experienced.

I told the pastor, "I know you planned on my speaking tonight, but I just can't do it. I have no idea what's wrong, but this pain is unbearable. I've never done this in my life," I admitted, "but I need for you to drive me to the nearest emergency room."

The pastor asked an associate minister to hold the service that night while he and Barbara rushed me to the nearest hospital.

The minute we walked in, a medical assistant asked, "On a scale of one to ten, how bad is it hurting?"

"I'm off the chart!" I grimaced.

I COULD HARDLY BREATHE

Three hours later, I was still writhing in agony and had yet to be examined. There were 40 or 50 other patients waiting for attention; gurneys lined the room, and people were everywhere.

In desperation, I made my way over to the triage nurse and said, "Look, I'm not sure what's wrong with me. I don't know if I have an appendix that's burst, or if I'm about to die. All I know is that I just cannot tolerate the pain any longer."

No sooner were those words out of my mouth than my breathing became extremely labored. It was a drop-to-your-knees kind of pain.

CRYING TO GOD

Since early that afternoon, Barbara had been praying for me—and now the pastor and the entire church were united in prayer. I, too, was calling out to God for healing. "Please, Lord, take the pain away," I prayed.

I thought of blind Bartimaeus crying out, *"Jesus, thou Son of David, have mercy on me"* (Mark 10:47 KJV). Believe me, I was echoing his words. At one point, I looked at Barbara and said, "I'm not sure I am going to make it!"

Finally, I was ushered in to see a doctor and his assistant. They drew blood and quickly gave me a couple of tests.

At that moment, lying on the hospital bed, I began to think about my situation and reflect on everything I had learned about faith, belief, hope, patience, and the Sovereignty of God. I knew that the Word tells us, *"Be anxious for nothing"* (Philippians 4:6), yet it is difficult to put this into practice when you are suffering.

I said, "Lord, I've done everything I know to do. If You heal me, and I trust You will—I will praise You." Then I added, "But if this is my time to go, and if this is the way of Your choosing, I am leaving it in Your hands."

THE UNKNOWN

Half an hour later, the doctor came in with the news: "Mr. Cerullo, you have a kidney stone. That's the problem."

He immediately ordered some morphine for my pain, and for the first time in more than ten hours, I felt relief.

The doctor gave me a prescription, and we flew back to Charlotte, North Carolina. I immediately saw a urologist, who determined I had a huge kidney stone that could not be passed or broken up by a laser. It could only be removed by surgery.

I still brag to Barbara, "I know what I went through was worse than childbirth. I just know it!" She just laughs.

When I look back on that day in Montreal, I know my physical discomfort was real, but my anxiety was the result of fear of the unknown.

That's exactly what takes place in so many areas of our lives—we become overwhelmed with worry because we have no idea what tomorrow holds.

I realize how difficult this is to do, yet God's Word tells us, *"Be anxious for nothing, but in everything by prayer and supplication with thanksgiving let your requests be made known to God"* (Philippians 4:6).

What the Lord taught me through this troubling time had an important impact on my life: Regardless of what happens, we must still trust God.

When we don't understand why, we must remember that we simply cannot see as God sees. We all fear the unknown, but take heart…the outcome is in the hands of our loving Father. He knows what is best for us.

THE TRAP

Troubled times can cause you to doubt the Lord's provision and question His love. They can paralyze your faith until you can't seem to reach out to the Lord to receive what you need.

Far too often, the trials of life turn our focus away from God and on our circumstances. We look to the world or to others instead of to the only Power that can deliver us.

Before we realize it, worry can stunt our faith and expectation and put a stranglehold on what God has placed in our hearts. Jesus declares, *"The worries of the world, and the deceitfulness of riches, and the desires for other things enter in and choke the word, and it becomes unfruitful"* (Mark 4:19)

Paul tells the Believers in Rome that God is the Potter, and we are the clay. *"Shall the thing formed say to him that formed it, why hast thou made me thus? Hath not the potter power over the clay?"* (Romans 9:20-21 KJV).

God is sovereign, and we are here for His good pleasure. The troubled times in our lives can only be heightened when we resist the work of God to make us like Christ.

I trust you are beginning to see why I want you to recognize the signs of tension and stress the moment they begin to appear.

Keep your eyes on Jesus. Your answer is on the way!

KING DAVID'S TURNAROUND

Earlier, we left King David crying himself to sleep. Yet he doesn't remain overwhelmed by self-pity and depression. Continue reading the Psalms, and here's what you'll discover:

God is near and capable of delivering you.

"But You, O LORD, be not far off; O You my help, hasten to my assistance" (Psalm 22:19).

You may fall down, but you don't have to stay down!

"When he falls, he will not be hurled headlong, because the LORD is the One who holds his hand" (Psalm 37:24).

The Lord will calm your anxieties.

"I lay down and slept; I awoke, for the LORD sustains me. I will not be afraid of ten thousands of people, who have set themselves against me round about" (Psalm 3:5-6).

Despite the injuries and insults King David had endured, he was able to step back from the brink of despair and praise God before his family, his countrymen, and ultimately the entire world. *"I will tell of Your name to my brethren; in the midst of the assembly I will praise You"* (Psalm 22:22).

PRESSING ON

What about Paul? Does he throw up his hands in defeat because he is persecuted, beaten, and thrown in prison? Far from it! The Apostle reminded the Believers at Philippi of these truths:

Look forward, not backward.

"Brethren," he declares, *"I count not myself to have apprehended: but this one thing I do, forgetting those things which are behind, and reaching forth unto those things which are before, I press toward the mark for the prize of the high calling of God in Christ Jesus"* (Philippians 3:13-14 KJV).

You have hidden strength.

"I can do all things through Christ which strengtheneth me" (Philippians 4:13 KJV).

Regardless of the situation, you can still praise God.

"Rejoice in the Lord always; again I will say, rejoice!" (Philippians 4:4)

THE DIVINE ANSWER

Today, take comfort in the fact that Jesus sees exactly what is happening in your life—every heartache, every sorrow, and every tear.

Stop being anxious about earthly concerns.

In His Sermon on the Mount, Jesus reveals the secret of living without worry. He declares, *"Do not be worried about your life, as to what you will eat or what you will drink; nor for your body, as to what you will put on. Is not life more than food, and the body more than clothing? Look at the birds of the air, that they do not sow, nor reap nor gather into barns, and yet your heavenly Father feeds them.*

Are you not worth much more than they? And who of you by being worried can add a single hour to his life?" (Matthew 6:25-27)

Start by seeking God.

Jesus gives us the Divine answer for all of our needs: *"But seek first His kingdom and His righteousness, and all these things will be added to you. So do not worry about tomorrow; for tomorrow will care for itself. Each day has enough trouble of its own* (vs. 33-34).

These are not the words of a noted psychologist or a popular self-help guru. This is the Son of God speaking directly to your heart—telling you to stop worrying and start living.

Ask the Lord to give you His eternal perspective on your circumstances so you will turn your eyes upon Him.

FIRST THINGS FIRST

Some may tell you that troubled times will just disappear through positive thinking or a better mental attitude. However, the true answer is found in a heart-changing experience.

God is waiting to offer His comfort and encouragement, but first you need to settle the most important question of your life. Have you asked Christ to come into your heart to forgive you of your sins? Have you acknowledged Him as your Savior and Lord?

If not, I am asking you to pause this moment and speak these words to Him from your heart:

Lord Jesus, I come before You now, asking You to forgive me of my sins. Come into my heart and be the Lord and Savior of my life. I believe that You died on the Cross and shed Your blood for my sins. I believe that on the third day You rose from the grave, conquering death and hell for all eternity. I accept You as my Savior and know that I will live eternally with You. Lord, create in me a strong desire to spend time in prayer and study Your Word that I may grow and mature in my faith. Thank you for transforming my life and making me a new creation in You.

Thank You, Lord!

Once the question of your salvation has been settled, everything about your future is going to change. You can rejoice in the fact that your past is forever buried, and you are now a child of the King!

YOUR TRANSFORMATION

Today, through words the Lord has inspired me to share with you, we begin a journey of hope and expectation. I believe God wants you to exchange life's pressures for the peace of mind that only He can bring.

Your Divine Transformation can begin this moment.

MY PRAYER FOR YOU:

Heavenly Father, You are the God of all comfort. Please extend Your arms of love around Your child. I pray that You will lift the heavy burdens they are carrying. And I am asking for the Presence of Your Holy Spirit to become real in their life as You calm their troubled heart. In Jesus' name. Amen.

IT IS WELL WITH MY SOUL

When peace like a river attendeth my way,
When sorrows like sea-billows roll;
Whatever my lot, Thou hast taught me to say,
"It is well, it is well with my soul."

And, Lord, haste the day when the faith shall be sight,
The clouds be rolled back as a scroll.
The trump shall resound and the Lord shall descend,
"Even so"—it is well with my soul.

—HORATIO G. SPAFFORD

CHAPTER TWO

The Spirit of Fear

IT WAS DARK ON THE BOEING 747. We had been flying over the Atlantic Ocean for more than three hours on our way from New York City to Rio de Janeiro.

I was traveling to Brazil to assist in an evangelistic outreach my father Morris Cerullo was conducting.

Most of the passengers were already bedded down for the night, except for me—I was wide awake. With my head propped up against a pillow, I was staring out the window just behind the wing on the right side of the aircraft. The night was black—no cities, no lights flickering below.

Suddenly, a bright yellow-orange flame began spewing from one of the engines, and my heart skipped a beat. This wasn't an illusion; I could see it with my own eyes. The fire was burning brightly.

For a split second, a flood of panic swept over me. "Is this plane okay? Are we going to crash into the sea?" I wondered.

Those troubling thoughts were quickly replaced with peace when the Lord reminded me of His Word: *"My peace I give to you; not as the world gives do I give to you. Do not let your heart be troubled, nor let it be fearful"* (John 14:27); and, *"Let the peace of Christ rule in your hearts"* (Colossians 3:15).

That's exactly what I did, and immediately I was enveloped by His peace.

Instead of alerting my fellow passengers or running to the galley to report what I had seen to a flight attendant, I felt led to stay where I was and pray.

THE PILOT SPOKE

Within a matter of moments, the fire began to diminish, and then completely disappeared. I thought, "That's incredible. There must be an automatic fire extinguisher next to the engine that kicked in."

Immediately, the pilot started a slow turn and then several minutes later calmly spoke on the public address system. "Ladies and gentlemen," he began, "we are experiencing difficulty with one of our engines and are returning to JFK Airport. Everything will be all right. We will let you know when we are ready to land." He didn't mention one word about the fire.

I shudder to think how the passengers would have reacted if they all had seen the flames or if the pilot had gone into elaborate details concerning the problem he was facing.

The moment the plane safely touched down in New York, I closed my eyes and offered a prayer of praise. "Thank You, Lord, for watching over us."

Did that experience cause me to stop flying? Absolutely not! I have taken hundreds of flights since—with the assurance that my life rests in God's hands.

I like the words of Ralph Waldo Emerson, who observed, "The wise man in the storm prays to God, not for safety from danger, but for deliverance from fear. It is the storm within that endangers him, not the storm without."

FEARS AND PHOBIAS

If I asked you to make a list called "My Three Greatest Fears," what would you include? Perhaps you would write...

...I am worried about my finances.
...I am afraid about the future of my family.
...I am anxious about my health.

Millions have a condition that goes far beyond simply being afraid. They have what psychiatrists call phobias: labels put on conditions they can't explain. There are hundreds of them, including:

- Aviophobia: fear of flying
- Enochlophobia: fear of crowds
- Pyrophobia: fear of fire
- Aerophobia: fear of drafts
- Tonitrophobia: fear of thunder

Perhaps the ultimate condition is phobophobia: fear of being afraid!

PANIC AND DREAD

One person, suffering from a phobia, describes her feelings this way: "My heart starts beating so fast—it feels like it's going to explode. My throat closes and I can't breathe. I start to choke. My hands begin sweating. I get so dizzy I have to hold onto the furniture or the wall to keep from falling or fainting. I know I'm going to die. I want to run, but I don't know where."

The National Institute of Mental Health has reported that between five and twelve percent of Americans complain of these conditions.

Later in this chapter, I want to tell you about the *real* cause of fear.

GODLY FEAR

The subject of fear is addressed throughout the Bible. So you may ask, "If fear is such a negative, why does the Bible instruct us to fear God?"

The Word declares, *"The fear of the Lord is the beginning of knowledge"* (Proverbs 1:7).

- Joseph says, *"Do this and live, for I fear God"* (Genesis 42:18).
- David writes, *"But as for me, I will come into Thy house in the multitude of Thy mercy: and in Thy fear will I worship toward Thy holy temple"* (Psalm 5:7 KJV).
- God says to Satan, *"Have you considered My servant Job? For there is no one like him on the earth, a*

blameless and upright man, fearing God and turning away from evil" (Job 1:8)

- Even the early Christians were described as *"going on in the fear of the Lord and in the comfort of the Holy Spirit"* (Acts 9:31).

Our fear of the Almighty is not an expression of fright or impending doom. In fact, it's just the opposite. As you see in these verses, Godly fear is based on reverence and respect.

IN BONDAGE

Two kinds of fear exist—healthy and unhealthy. For example, it is a good fear that keeps us from driving 100 miles an hour, from standing too near the edge of a cliff, or from placing our hand on a hot stove.

However, we need to differentiate between the *emotion* of fear and the *spirit* of fear. The first is God-given and helps protect us. The second is from Satan and is designed by him to place us in bondage. That's what Paul is talking about when he says, *"God hath not given us the spirit of fear; but of power, and of love, and of a sound mind"* (2 Timothy 1:7 KJV).

Just as God sends His angels as ministering spirits, so the devil sends his demons—fallen angels. One offers life; the other death.

Solomon writes, *"The fear of the LORD is the beginning of wisdom"* (Proverbs 9:10 KJV). This is clearly a healthy, God-given fear. In fact, this reverence is a covering for us. The Father calls us to holiness and a hatred of evil—not to be "politically correct," but to have a holy respect that moves us to purity and obedience. This is God's way of leading us to peace and freedom.

As a Believer, you have been liberated—set free! *"For you have not received a spirit of slavery leading to fear again, but you have received a spirit of adoption as sons by which we cry out, "Abba! Father!"* (Romans 8:15)

This liberty refers to God as a Daddy, Who delights in protecting and comforting His children.

THE ETERNAL CONFLICT

Your battle against fear is not a physical confrontation: It is spiritual.

There are two forces at work in this world. You might think of them as light and darkness or good and evil. Call them what you will, they are very simply God and Satan.

The Bible clearly tells us to put on the whole armor of God, *"that ye may be able to stand against the wiles of the devil. For we wrestle not against flesh and blood, but against principalities, against powers, against the rulers of the darkness of this world, against spiritual wickedness in high places"* (Ephesians 6:11-12 KJV).

If this sounds fictional to you, believe me, it is very real. The spirit world may be invisible to your eyes, yet it is just as natural as the world in which you and I live.

Rejoice that you have won the victory in the battle against your soul by calling on the name of Jesus. When you asked Christ to forgive your sins and come into your heart, He did just that. Jesus now lives inside you. He has delivered you from the kingdom of darkness and translated you into the Kingdom of His Son (Colossians 1:12-14).

The issue of spiritual warfare is one I will refer to several times in this book. I believe it lies at the heart of defeating anxiety and overcoming the troubled times in your life.

DON'T HARM YOUR TEMPLE!

Let me share two reasons fear should have no place in your life:

1. Fear denies the truth of Scripture.

The moment you allow earthly trepidation to determine your behavior, you are in direct conflict with the Word of God that proclaims, *"I will never desert you, nor will I ever forsake you"* (Hebrews 13:5).

I want to encourage you to replace fear with faith. Believe the Word when it says that God has all power in Heaven and on earth. He does! He desires only the best for you.

2. Fear causes harm to the temple of God.

The instant you are born again, the Almighty miraculously takes residence in your body: *"Do you not know that you are a temple of God and that the Spirit of God dwells in you?"* (1 Corinthians 3:16); and, *"Because you are sons, God has sent forth the Spirit of His Son into our hearts"* (Galatians 4:6).

Don't permit anxiety and fear to invade the temple of God—which is in your body.

Medical research has proven beyond doubt that worry can cause heart trouble, high blood pressure, ulcers, stomach disorders and more. If fear is damaging your body—it is also destroying what God has placed within you.

And something more...I believe fear is in direct conflict with your Christian testimony. Jesus declares, *"Let your light shine before men in such a way that they may see your good works, and glorify your Father who is in heaven"* (Matthew 5:16).

God, in His kindness, stands ready to forgive, to heal your troubled spirit, to strengthen your heart, and to give you victory!

YOUR ARK OF SAFETY

Certainly, we must take every human precaution necessary to shield our families from danger, yet the Lord is our only Source of complete safety.

The Word affirms that through faith, we *"are kept by the power of God"* (1 Peter 1:5 KJV). *"For in the time of trouble He shall hide me safe in His pavilion: in the secret of His tabernacle shall He hide me; He shall set me upon a rock"* (Psalm 27:5 KJV).

PROTECTED BY THE WORD

What is your greatest weapon against fear? The mighty Word of God.

Let me share 15 Scriptures I would like you to commit to memory. I encourage you to make a copy of these pages and place the verses on your refrigerator or the dashboard of your car.

Read them aloud day after day until the words find a home in your heart and saturate your thoughts and spirit.

1. I will keep my mind on Christ.

"Thou wilt keep him in perfect peace, whose mind is stayed on Thee, because he trusteth in Thee" (Isaiah 26:3 KJV).

2. The Lord will give me strength.

"Do not fear, for I am with you; do not anxiously look about you, for I am your God. I will strengthen you, surely I will help you, surely I will uphold you with My righteous right hand" (Isaiah 41:10).

3. God is holding my hand.

"I am the LORD your God, who upholds your right hand, Who says to you, 'Do not fear, I will help you'" (Isaiah 41:13).

4. I will trust the Lord.

"When I am afraid, I will put my trust in You. In God, whose word I praise, in God I have put my trust; I shall not be afraid. What can mere man do to me?" (Psalm 56:3-4)

5. I will not be afraid.

"The LORD is my light and my salvation; whom shall I fear? The LORD is the strength of my life; of whom shall I be afraid?" (Psalm 27:1 KJV)

6. I will be confident.

"Though a host encamp against me, my heart will not fear; though war arise against me, in spite of this I shall be confident" (Psalm 27:3)

7. God is on my side.

"The LORD is for me; I will not fear; what can man do to me?" (Psalm 118:6)

8. My Father knows all about me.

"Indeed, the very hairs of your head are all numbered. Do not fear; you are more valuable than many sparrows" (Luke 12:7)

9. God is my salvation.

"Behold, God is my salvation, I will trust and not be afraid; for the LORD GOD is my strength and song, and He has become my salvation" (Isaiah 12:2).

10. The Lord will be with me.

"Do not fear, for I have redeemed you; I have called you by name; you are Mine! When you pass through the waters, I will be with you; and through the rivers, they will not overflow you. When you walk through the fire, you will not be scorched, nor will the flame burn you" (Isaiah 43:1-2).

11. God will not fail me.

"Be strong and courageous, do not be afraid or tremble at them, for the LORD your God is the one who goes with you. He will not fail you or forsake you" (Deuteronomy 31:6).

12. I will not be dismayed.

"'You need not fight in this battle; station yourselves, stand and see the salvation of the LORD on your behalf, O Judah and Jerusalem.' Do not fear or be dismayed; tomorrow go out to face them, for the LORD is with you" (2 Chronicles 20:17).

13. I will replace fear with God's perfect love.

"There is no fear in love; but perfect love casts out fear" (1 John 4:18).

14. I am secure in God's hands.

"The fear of man bringeth a snare: but whoso putteth his trust in the LORD shall be safe" (Proverbs 29:25 KJV).

15. I will rest in the Lord.

"When you lie down, you will not be afraid; When you lie down, your sleep will be sweet" (Proverbs 3:24).

Now you are armed for battle! The next time Satan attempts to launch his arrows of fear and his darts of doubt, boldly begin to speak the Word and watch him flee!

MY PRAYER FOR YOU

Heavenly Father, in the Name of Jesus, I pray that from this day forward, the mind of Your child will be free from worry and fear and that faith will arise in their heart. I pray that by Your Almighty Power, You will remove any spirit of anxiety that has taken up residence within them. May You give them Your love that casts out all fear. May Your Peace that surpasses all understanding guard their heart and mind during their times of trouble.
In Jesus' name. Amen.

FAITH IS THE VICTORY

Encamped along the hills of light,
Ye Christian soldiers rise,
And press the battle ere the night
Shall veil the glowing skies,
Against the foe in vales below,
Let all our strength be hurled;
Faith is the victory, we know,
That overcomes the world.

Faith is the victory!
Faith is the victory!
O, Glorious victory,
That overcomes the world.
—JOHN H. YATES

CHAPTER THREE

When Bad Things Happen to God's People

Rabbi Harold Kushner wrote a bestselling book *When Bad Things Happen to Good People.* I'd like to change the last two words from "Good People" to "God's People."

Why would a kind, loving Heavenly Father allow tragedy to strike one of His children? How could a born-again Believer, who is living an obedient, righteous life, experience tragedy after tragedy?

Perhaps the most perplexing question many Christians ponder is, "Why?"

- Why is my family being torn apart?
- Why is my health failing?
- Why is my financial outlook so bleak?

There are many reasons God's children suffer. At the outset, we must understand that the difficulties of life are not optional. Times of trouble will happen. As Paul writes to Timothy, *"Indeed, all who desire to live godly in Christ Jesus will be persecuted"* (2 Timothy 3:12). Jesus declares that God *"causes His sun to rise on the evil and the good, and sends rain on the righteous and the unrighteous"* (Matthew 5:45).

A MAN OF INTEGRITY

I believe that at least once every year, we all need to read the Book of Job. Here is a man of impeccable character—one who was highly respected, extremely successful, and enjoyed a loving family.

In a confrontation between God and Satan, the devil was searching for someone to test. The Lord asks, *"Have you considered My servant Job? For there is no one like him on the earth, a blameless and upright man, fearing God and turning away from evil"* (Job 1:8).

From the outset, we know that God permitted what happened next. Job was stripped of every earthly possession—including his family. He even lost his health. As he describes it, *"My flesh is clothed with worms and a crust of dirt, my skin hardens and runs. My days are swifter than a weaver's shuttle, and come to an end without hope"* (Job 7:5-6).

Satan was convinced that in this broken condition, Job would curse God and die. But Job didn't.

- Job never blames the Almighty.
- Job never turns his back on God.
- Job never loses his faith.

Was Job distressed about his situation? Absolutely. His human emotions were no different than yours and mine. At one point, *"Job arose and tore his robe and shaved his head, and he fell to the ground"* (Job 1:20).

However, this desperate man was not writhing in anger. There, flat on his face before God, the Bible says that he *"worshiped"* (v. 20), telling the Lord, *"Naked I came from my mother's womb, and naked I shall return there. The Lord gave and the Lord has taken away. Blessed be the name of the Lord"* (v. 21). Despite all of the suffering he endured, *"Job did not sin nor did he blame God"* (v. 22).

DEVASTATING NEWS

How do you respond when catastrophe strikes?

I recall the day I was in a hotel room at a convention when Barbara phoned me with some news that was absolutely devastating. I came within a breath of asking, "God, why are You letting this happen to me? Why don't you go ahead and take my life now?"

What kept my sanity and prevented me from doing something irrational? All I had learned from the Word and my walk with God suddenly swept through my mind and heart. Remembering the story of Job, I said, *"Though he slay me, yet will I trust in him"* (Job 13:15 KJV).

Job didn't understand spiritual warfare as taught in the New Testament, yet I believe he perceived there was a greater battle taking place. He knew that life consisted of much more than what he saw—or what he possessed.

Remember, this was a confrontation between God and Satan, and Job was the test case.

"AS GOLD"

Job's confidence in the Lord was so strong that, regardless of his agony, he was willing to place himself completely in the hands of the Father. He didn't know when or how deliverance would arrive, but he knew that God was still God: *"He knows the way I take; when He has tried me, I shall come forth as gold"* (Job 23:10).

If you want to know the answer to the question "Why?" read Job 38-41. It's the longest speech from God recorded in Scripture.

The Lord is telling Job, "Here is how things work in the world I have created—and I have all authority in Heaven and on earth." That's all Job needed to know.

What a contrast between the first and last chapters of this dramatic account. God does restore Job—blessing him with twice as much as he had before Satan's onslaught. The Lord even extends his life another 140 years.

GOD'S PURPOSE FOR US

We need to be diligent in keeping our focus on why we have been placed on this earth. The Almighty desires to transform us into His image—to make the kingdoms of this world the Kingdom of our God. He is refining, shaping, and building us with His character and depositing within us His nature.

We are all ministers of God—not just the pastor who stands behind a pulpit on Sunday. Instead of being "spoon-fed" with bite-size morsels of encouragement once a week, we will be sustained when we open God's Word every day and delve with delight into its truths and treasures.

Your greatest preparation for times of trouble includes feeding and digesting Scripture until it is deep in your heart and evident in a walk that reflects His peace.

"WEAPONS OF RIGHTEOUSNESS"

Paul is able to endure appalling hardships and suffering because he has *"weapons of righteousness."* He writes:

"But in everything commending ourselves as servants of God, in much endurance, in afflictions, in hardships, in distresses, in beatings, in imprisonments, in tumults, in labors, in sleeplessness, in hunger, in purity, in knowledge, in patience, in kindness, in the Holy Spirit, in genuine love, in the word of truth, in the power of God; by the weapons of righteousness for the right hand and the left, by glory and dishonor, by evil report and good report; regarded as deceivers and yet true; as unknown yet well-known, as dying yet behold, we live; as punished yet not put to death, as sorrowful yet always rejoicing, as poor yet making many rich, as having nothing yet possessing all things" (2 Corinthians 6:4-10).

What a marvelous testimony! And the Word has this example for you and me: *"If the Spirit of Him who raised Jesus from the dead dwells in you, He who raised Christ Jesus from the dead will also give life to your mortal bodies through His Spirit who dwells in you"* (Romans 8:11).

So rejoice and believe—even in your hardships. Because He lives, so shall you.

NINE REASONS

Here are nine answers to the question, "Why do bad things happen to God's people?"

1. Because of God's purpose for our lives.

Don't be discouraged. There is always a reason behind every calamity: *"For it is God who is at work in you, both to will and to work for His good pleasure"* (Philippians 2:13).

When desperation is your only thought, realize that God has a step-by-step plan and purpose that will take you from crisis to triumph. Scripture declares that we glory in tribulation, *"knowing that tribulation brings about perseverance; and perseverance, proven character; and proven character, hope; and hope does not disappoint, because the love of God has been poured out within our hearts through the Holy Spirit who was given to us"* (Romans 5:3-5). Trials build our character and make us strong.

Have you ever watched a butterfly fight to make its way out of the cocoon? It's in the struggle for freedom that its wings are strengthened.

The psalmist declares, *"You have tried us, O God; You have refined us as silver is refined"* (Psalm 66:10). The Father permits us to walk through adversity to produce quality and character in our lives. He wants to transform us into the likeness of Christ.

2. Because of Satan's attacks.

As a Christian, you're living in the devil's battle zone—always in his crosshairs. The Word tells us, *"Be of sober spirit, be on the alert. Your adversary, the devil, prowls around like a roaring lion, seeking someone to devour"* (1 Peter 5:8).

Satan comes to *"steal and kill and destroy"* (John 10:10). But remember, *"Greater is he that is in you, than he that is in the world"* (1 John 4:4 KJV).

Our lives will be tested by fire. What is made of wood, hay, or stubble will burn. I pray the trials will produce something of far greater value—gold and precious jewels to lay at the feet of Jesus when we enter Heaven (1 Corinthians 3:12-13).

3. Because of the consequences of our own sin.

The moment Adam and Eve disobeyed the Creator and ate fruit from the forbidden tree, sin entered into mankind—and because of their act, we suffer pain until this day. It was the beginning of the curse (Genesis 3:14-19).

Our sin creates a breach in our fellowship with the Father. *"But your iniquities have made a separation between you and your God"* (Isaiah 59:2).

Thanks be to God for providing a way of escape by sending His Son, Jesus, to die on the Cross for you and me.

4. Because of the sins of others.

The world will never erase the tragedy of September 11, 2001. Did all those in the Twin Towers, at the Pentagon, or the passengers on four hijacked airliners deserve to die? Of course not. Many were God-fearing, Bible-believing Christians.

Does a wife deserve to be abused by her husband? Do parents deserve to lose a child to a drunk driver? Because of the sinful decisions made by others, we may suffer greatly.

I've been asked, "Why doesn't God step in and prevent someone from blowing up a building or murdering an innocent victim?"

God has created us as free moral agents with the liberty to make our own choices. That freedom gives us the right to choose evil over good—even inflicting pain on others.

If you've ever suffered because of other people's choices, Jesus knows. *"For consider Him who has endured such hostility by sinners against Himself, so that you will not grow weary and lose heart"* (Hebrews 12:3).

He experienced pain and torment because of the sins of others, but He kept trusting in His Father, Who is faithful. So must we.

5. Because of God's permission.

The account of Job is a case in point. The Lord *allowed* a time of great testing—He did not cause it.

It is not for us to question God's decisions: *"For as the heavens are higher than the earth, so are My ways higher than your ways, and My thoughts than your thoughts"* (Isaiah 55:9).

As Paul declares, *"Oh, the depth of the riches both of the wisdom and knowledge of God! How unsearchable are His judgments and unfathomable His ways"* (Romans 11:33). You may sometimes struggle to understand why God permits testing and times of trouble, but He has great rewards for those who hold fast to their faith.

6. Because of God's desire that we know our own hearts.

The children of Israel grew bored. They were tired of eating manna and sweltering in the wilderness. Many complained, "Oh that we could return to Egypt."

God knew exactly the condition of their hearts—yet He wanted them to be honest with themselves. That's why He allowed them to endure such hardships.

Read these powerful words: *"You shall remember all the way which the LORD your God has led you in the wilderness these forty years, that He might humble you, testing you, to know what was in your heart, whether you would keep His commandments or not"* (Deuteronomy 8:2).

Later, the Almighty says, *"For the LORD your God is testing you to find out if you love the LORD your God with all your heart and with all your soul"* (Deuteronomy 13:3).

Beloved, God in His kindness sprinkles our lives with tests that give us a chance to love Him above self and circumstances.

7. Because of God's love for us.

When they are about to discipline a disobedient child, parents often will say, "This is going to hurt me more than it will hurt you," and for loving parents, this is true.

It's the same with God. Because He loves us, He corrects us: *"My son, do not regard lightly the discipline of the*

Lord, nor faint when you are reproved by Him; for those whom the Lord loves He disciplines, and He scourges every son whom He receives" (Hebrews 12:5-6).

We understand what is right, yet often fail to act accordingly—and we must live with the consequences.

The Word declares, *"Do not be deceived, God is not mocked; for whatever a man sows, this he will also reap. For the one who sows to his own flesh will from the flesh reap corruption, but the one who sows to the Spirit will from the Spirit reap eternal life"* (Galatians 6:7-8).

If you're not enjoying a harvest of peace, ask God for forgiveness, and He will joyfully restore you. Never forget: *YOU ARE LOVED!*

8. Because of the Lord's desire that we enter into the fellowship of His suffering.

Can you identify with the pain and agony of Calvary? Have you been bonded with Christ in what He endured on the Cross?

Scripture declares, *"If we suffer, we shall also reign with him"* (2 Timothy 2:12 KJV). Even when we are unfaithful, the Lord remains faithful—for He cannot deny Himself.

Develop an attitude like the Apostle Paul, who declares, *"For I consider that the sufferings of this present time are not worthy to be compared with the glory that is to be revealed to us"* (Romans 8:18), and. *"For momentary, light affliction is producing for us an eternal weight of glory far beyond all comparison"* (2 Corinthians 4:17).

Remember, the fellowship of His suffering brings honor and glory to God: *"In this you greatly rejoice, even though now for a little while, if necessary, you have been distressed by various trials, so that the proof of your faith, being more precious than gold which is perishable, even though tested by fire, may be found to result in praise and glory and honor at the revelation of Jesus Christ"* (1 Peter 1:6-7).

When times of trouble come, rejoice! Give glory to the Father. As James wrote, *"Consider it all joy, my brethren, when you encounter various trials, knowing that the testing of your faith produces endurance. And let endurance have its perfect result, so that you may be perfect and complete, lacking in nothing"* (James 1:2-4).

The Bible tell us, *"Although He was a Son, He learned obedience from the things which He suffered"* (Hebrews 5:8). If suffering was a part of God's preparation process for Jesus' sacrifice for us, then how much more do sinful people's lives need to be tempered by trials!

There is joy in identifying with the sufferings of Jesus.

9. Because God wants to teach us.

The lessons the Father shares with us through pain and suffering are for our ultimate benefit.

"He disciplines us for our good, so that we may share His holiness. All discipline for the moment seems not to be joyful, but sorrowful; yet to those who have been trained by it, afterwards it yields the peaceful fruit of righteousness" (Hebrews 12:10-11).

Adopt the view of the psalmist: *"It is good for me that I was afflicted, that I may learn Your statutes"* (Psalm 119:71). He also wrote, *"Blessed is the man whom You chasten, O LORD, and whom You teach out of Your law; that You may grant him relief from the days of adversity"* (Psalm 94:12-13).

This is the desire of God's heart—to ease your burden and lighten the load you are carrying. Ask the Lord for discernment concerning these nine reasons as they apply to your circumstances.

THREE CHOICES

When times of trouble come your way, don't question, "Where is God?" Instead, ask, "Where am *I*?"

Troubling times are not a *reflection* of your spiritual character or condition. They are a *measurement* of them. We cannot always alter our circumstances, yet we can change the way we respond to them.

How will you react when tough times arrive? You have three choices:

1. You can play the blame game—shifting the cause of your problems to God or others.
2. You can have a pity party, feeling sorry for yourself in the midst of trouble.
3. You can place your complete trust in God, saying, "Regardless of what happens, Lord, I'm going to serve You."

"ALL THINGS"

If you find yourself trapped in the pressure-cooker of life, start quoting this verse every hour, if necessary: *"We know that all things work together for good to them that love God, to them who are the called according to his purpose"* (Romans 8:28 KJV).

When you are a child of God and called by Him, you can boldly claim that promise. *All* things—the good and the bad—are working according to His master plan.

There's hope on the horizon! Jesus says, *"In the world you have tribulation, but take courage; I have overcome the world"* (John 16:33).

Rest in the assurance that *"the sufferings of this present time are not worthy to be compared with the glory that is to be revealed in us"* (Romans 8:18).

What a comfort to know that you are never alone when you cry. God is there when you are troubled, waiting to wrap His loving arms around you saying, "Do not be anxious or afraid. Trust Me. I love you and am working all things for your good."

MY PRAYER FOR YOU

Heavenly Father, although we don't always understand why You allow pain, suffering, and anxiety to enter our lives, please help Your child to rest in the assurance that You are working all things for their good. Thank You for Your unfailing love and tender mercy.
In Jesus' name. Amen.

TURN YOUR EYES UPON JESUS

Turn your eyes upon Jesus,
Look full in His wonderful face,
And the things of earth
will grow strangely dim,
In the Light of His glory and grace.

– HELEN H. LEMMEL

CHAPTER FOUR

You Can Defeat the Strategies of Satan!

DURING THE SUMMER MONTHS between high school and college, I had the privilege of traveling to Madras, India, to be a part of one of my dad's overseas crusades.

Over 100,000 people packed the soccer grounds each night—a huge crusade by American standards, but rather small compared to many of the meetings Dad has conducted in India. Several of his crusades in that nation attracted crowds of 400,000 and 500,000 people.

The raised platform we constructed on one side of the grounds was typical of the physical arrangement needed for Dad's meetings. In front was a large roped off area where people could come forward after he prayed the prayer of faith for healing. There, those who believed they had received a miracle from God could share their testimony with one of the personal workers or counselors.

For example, "Sir, you say you were deaf," a team member would say through an interpreter. "I want you to place your finger in your good ear and let me see if you can hear out of your bad ear."

As the testimonies were validated, the person who was healed was ushered to the platform, where they testified to the huge throng about what had just taken place. It built the faith of others when they saw that God's Presence and healing power was alive in their midst. The Lord received all the glory!

"DAVID, GET DOWN THERE!"

One night during the Madras crusade, I was sitting at the audio control board, when an elderly woman, just a few feet away from the roped off section, began screaming right in the middle of my dad's sermon. She was extremely loud—almost deafening to those around her—and very disruptive.

To make matters worse, the woman began rolling on the ground, foaming at the mouth, and ripping off her clothes.

My father stopped preaching for less than ten seconds. He leaned over the railing and made eye contact with me at the side of the platform. Pointing to the screaming woman, he ordered, "David, get down there and use what you know in the name of Jesus!" He then continued his message.

A SMALL PROBLEM

Immediately, I walked over to the woman who was very frail—just skin and bones! I estimated her to be in her eighties and weighing no more than seventy pounds. As I drew closer, I thought, "This isn't going to be a problem."

I had no fear at all when my father asked me to take charge of the situation. I was a young, athletic guy—quite strong for my age—and wasn't about to be intimidated by this small, out-of-control woman.

I WAS STUNNED!

She was still screaming and thrashing when I reached down to take hold of her. The woman couldn't speak a word of English, and I didn't know the Tamil language she was speaking. I thought, "In the worst case scenario, I can pick her up and physically remove her from the meeting."

Just as I bent over to reach her, the woman rolled again and her forearm hit me across the chest. As God is my witness, I flew through the air and landed at least six feet away—absolutely stunned, and breathless!

It was like playing football and being hit by a 280-pound lineman. I didn't just fall back, I was airborne—all 185 pounds of me!

SPIRITUAL WARFARE

Picking myself up, I initially was gripped by fear. "Oh, my Lord," I muttered, realizing that for the first time in my life, I was coming face to face with an unexpected, unseen force—it was satanic!

I dusted myself off and understood immediately why my father had said, "David, get down there and use what you know in the name of Jesus!" This woman was demon-possessed.

What did I know about spiritual warfare? I must confess, not a great deal. But Scriptures I had learned began to race through my mind and spirit:

- I knew that *"greater is he that is in you, than he that is in the world"* (1 John 4:4 KJV).
- I knew that *"Whatsoever ye shall bind on earth shall be bound in heaven: and whatsoever ye shall loose on earth shall be loosed in heaven"* (Matthew 18:18 KJV).
- I knew that Jesus says, *"In my name shall they cast out devils"* (Mark 16:17 KJV).

Several men came to my assistance to help restrain her, but this petite woman was tossing them off like flies. It took eight of us to finally subdue her to the point where we could begin to pray. Boldly, we began speaking to the devil, "Come out of her. In the name of Jesus, leave this woman now!"

In a matter of minutes, her satanic demeanor was replaced by complete peace. She quietly stood to her feet as if in a daze, unsure of what had just happened.

The woman looked at us as if to say, "Who are you? And why are you standing around me?"

She brushed herself off, fixed her dress, raised her hands toward Heaven, and began to speak in her native language. I grabbed an interpreter and asked, "What is she saying?"

He told me, "She is thanking and praising God for setting her free from the demons that have tormented her for so many years."

The service continued without skipping a beat.

I was just a teenager, yet—in the name of Jesus—I confronted Satan. Do you realize you have that same spiritual authority in Christ?

Beloved, just like me and all other Believers, you have an opportunity to "use what you know" in the name of Jesus. And when you do, make sure you are standing on the Word and dressed in the full armor of God.

WHO IS SATAN?

No one can convince me the devil isn't real. From both personal experience and God's Word, I know he definitely is.

Here are just a few of the facts the Bible tells us about Satan:

- He is a fallen angel who rebelled against the Creator (Isaiah 14:12-15; Ezekiel 28:15).
- He is the father of lies (John 8:44).
- He afflicts us (Job 2:7).
- He is a deceiver (Revelation 12:9).
- He is powerful (Ephesians 2:2).
- He possesses unbelievers (Luke 22:3).
- His goal is to undo God's work (Mark 4:15).
- Christ will triumph over him (Luke 10:18).
- He will be rendered powerless (Hebrews 2:14)
- He will be destroyed and consigned to hell forever (Matthew 25:41).

STAND GUARD!

When I returned from India, I began to think about that encounter with Satan—and vowed that with God's grace, I would never allow the devil to gain a foothold in my life.

In ancient Israel, every city had a watchman, a sentry who stood guard at a specific post. That person's assignment, as the first line of defense, was to blow the trumpet and warn the other soldiers of an impending enemy attack.

God spoke to Ezekiel and said, *"Son of man, speak to the children of your people and say to them, 'If I bring a sword upon a land, and the people of the land take one man from among them and make him their watchman... but if the watchman sees the sword coming and does not blow the trumpet and the people are not warned, and a sword comes and takes a person from them, he is taken away in his iniquity; but his blood I will require from the watchman's hand.' Now as for you, son of man, I have appointed you a watchman for the house of Israel; so you will hear a message from My mouth and give them warning from Me"* (Ezekiel 33:2, 6-7).

As the people of God, we are to be *"the light of the world"* (Matthew 5:14).

Today, every Believer must become a sentinel, a watchman, ready to sound the alarm. Be vigilant! The moment you become distracted with earthly pursuits, the devil will launch his attacks of worry and anxiety.

The Word instructs us that after preparing for spirtual warfare, we must, *"With all prayer and petition pray at all times in the Spirit, and with this in view, be on the alert with all perseverance and petition for all the saints"* (Ephesians 6:18).

If we remain faithful at our post, the Lord will warn us of the well-timed attacks of the enemy, so that we can create a boundary of protection through prayer.

We don't need to be afraid of the devil, but rather we are to be aware of his schemes and vigilant to guard our hearts and minds.

THE DEVIL'S DEVICES

Satan is a cunning foe.

Paul, writing to the Believers at Corinth, encourages them to walk in a spirit of forgiveness: *"so that no advantage would be taken of us by Satan, for we are not ignorant of his schemes"* (2 Corinthians 2:11).

Let's examine this verse.

The word *"ignorant"* means to be "without knowledge or understanding of something." It is where we get our word "agnostic."

In our culture, we have defined an agnostic as a person who is unsure if he or she believes in God. In truth, however, an agnostic is someone who does not know or understand something—regardless of the subject.

Our English word "ignore" is taken from the same root word. In this verse, we're urged not to ignore —or be an agnostic without understanding—Satan's devices.

Paul warns that we should not let the devil take *"advantage"* of us. How true! Satan makes great strides against those who are unaware of his ways—leading to pervasive fear and anxiety in their lives.

The word *"schemes"* can be traced to a root word meaning "thoughts" and also implies "plans and plots."

When we combine these definitions, this verse can be interpreted in this way: to the degree we are ignorant of the way our adversary the devil thinks and operates unaware of his plans, plots, schemes, and devices to that degree he will prey on us, defraud us of what is ours, and will have or hold the greater portion of our lives.

THE LION'S SHARE

This angel of darkness greedily wants to sap the lion's share of your joy, your peace, your relationships, your physical body, your finances, and your spiritual life. He will use every tempting ploy possible to trouble and confuse your life with consternation and fear—and attempt to cause you to question God and His Word.

Here's the only conclusion we can draw: If God tells us we must not be ignorant of the devil's plans, surely He is willing to reveal them to us. Ask Him!

One of Satan's schemes is to bring times of trouble into your family, your health, and your finances. To the higher degree you walk in ignorance of the devil, the greater the foothold he will have and the more he will rob you of your blessings.

Spend time in the Word and on your knees. The Lord will illuminate your mind, cause you to be aware of the devil's devices, and quicken you to do battle.

ESCAPE THE SPIRAL!

I learned a valuable life lesson in the process of earning my pilot's license. The flight instructor told me the dangers of a downward spiral—when gravitational forces draw a plane closer and closer to the earth into a tight circle, your pace accelerates.

He cautioned, "David, it's really serious. You could start with a really wide spiral, then suddenly you are going faster and tighter until you slam into the ground."

He then explained how to escape from the deadly force: "You have to reduce the power, give the plane reverse rudder, pull on the yoke as hard as you can, and fly in the opposite direction of the spin." Then he added these ominous words: "If you don't do each of these things, you will crash and burn."

During my flight test, with an F.A.A. instructor seated in the cockpit next to me, the pilot purposely put us into such a spin and announced, "The plane's yours. Get us out of this!"

Of course, he was ready to take control if I forgot the drill in the heat of the moment, but I didn't. I reduced the power, reversed the rudder, and pulled on that yoke with every ounce of energy I could muster, and the plane was freed from impending danger.

The parallel to this story is that Satan can entrap us in his downward cycle until we are spinning dangerously out of control. The escape route is as simple as following God's instructions. Scripture tells us, *"It was for freedom that Christ set us free; therefore keep standing firm and do not be subject again to a yoke of slavery"* (Galatians 5:1).

My friend, the answer to many of your troubles simply is to take authority over the forces of Satan and stand in the victory that God declares in His Word. The Almighty is on your side!

DEFEATING THE ENEMY!

Many well-meaning Believers have permitted the Prince of Darkness to gain a foothold in their lives. He has marched in, taken over, and claimed territory for himself with hardly a struggle.

Recognize what is taking place. Don't become frightened. Since God is your Ally, bravely confront your adversary.

If Satan has a strategy, so must we. Let me spell out a five-step plan you can use effectively to vanquish the enemy:

Number One: Be aware of Satan's strategies.

You are asked to put on the whole armor of God— *"your loins girt about with truth...the breastplate of right-eousness...your feet shod with the preparation of the gospel of peace...taking the shield of faith...the helmet of salvation, and the sword of the Spirit, which is the word of God"* (Ephesians 6:14-17 KJV).

He wants to protect you with the Truth that will set you free! The Lord asks you to put on the breastplate that declares you are in right standing with the Father. He wants you to come prepared with the Gospel of Peace.

You are to hold up the shield of faith to protect yourself from the arrows of the enemy and put on the helmet of salvation to protect your mind from Satan's attacks. You must be armed with the sword of the Spirit—the mighty Word of God that declares you are more than a conqueror through Him who loves you.

Why is this necessary? Again, it is so that you *"will be able to stand firm against the schemes of the devil. For our struggle is not against flesh and blood, but against the rulers, against the powers, against the world forces of this darkness, against the spiritual forces of wickedness in the heavenly places"* (Ephesians 6:11-12).

Through Christ, you have the power to defeat Satan!

Number Two: Pray.

I am not asking you to become a one-person army and fight the devil alone. You need the Lord's help.

God has given you this promise: *"He will call upon Me, and I will answer him; I will be with him in trouble; I will rescue him and honor him"* (Psalm 91:15).

When you recite The Lord's Prayer, think carefully and prayerfully about the words. Believe it from your heart when you ask God to *"...deliver us from evil"* (Matthew 6:13).

Number Three: Wage spiritual warfare.

The Word will equip you with the artillery necessary to withstand Satan and his demons: *"For the weapons of our warfare are not carnal, but mighty through God to the pulling down of strong holds"* (2 Corinthians 10:4 KJV).

Be strong! With confidence in the Lord and His Word, stand up to Satan and rebuke his spirits of doubt, unbelief, and anxiety.

Number Four: Get "spiritually violent."

Jesus certainly didn't mince words when He confronted the devil. At the synagogue in Capernaum, a spirit was actually speaking through a demon-possessed man. The Bible records: "And Jesus rebuked him, saying, *'Be quiet, and come out of him!' Throwing him into convulsions, the unclean spirit cried out with a loud voice and came out of him"* (Mark 1:25-26).

You must aggressively counterattack Satan. Jesus declares, *"The kingdom of heaven suffereth violence, and the violent take it by force"* (Matthew 11:12 KJV).

Those words may sound scary, but remember, Jesus declares, *"I am with you always"* (Matthew 28:20)!

Number Five: Stay alert!

Become a spiritual watchman—for yourself and your family.

Jesus tells you to *"Keep on the alert at all times, praying that you may have strength to escape all these things that are about to take place, and to stand before the Son of Man"* (Luke 21:36).

"STAY OUT OF MY LIFE!"

Christ can free you from the chains and bondage of Satan. He promises, *"I am come that they might have life, and that they might have it more abundantly"* (John 10:10 KJV).

The Word declares, *"The Son of God appeared for this purpose, to destroy the works of the devil"* (1 John 3:8).

Turn your troubled times over to the One Who came to liberate you from the works of Satan—sin, sickness, and death: *"Submit therefore to God. Resist the devil and he will flee from you"* (James 4:7).

Oh, what a marvelous promise from the Lord! You don't have to be intimidated by Satan and his evil maneuvers. On the authority of God Himself, you can tell the devil, "Stay out of my life!" And he will take flight!

Now that's worth getting excited about!

MY PRAYER FOR YOU

Heavenly Father, please give Your child the discernment to recognize every ploy of the devil and the power to stand against him. I pray You will give them the courage and the will to submit themselves to You, because You are the only One Who can deliver them from evil. Today, I am believing with Your child for total victory over Satan, fully confident in the truth of Your Word that greater are You, Lord, in them, than he that is in the world!

In Jesus' name. Amen.

A MIGHTY FORTRESS

A mighty fortress is our God,
A bulwark never failing.
Our helper He amid the flood,
Of mortal ills prevailing.
For still our ancient foe,
Doth seek to work us woe,
His craft and power are great,
And armed with cruel hate,
On earth is not his equal.
And tho this world, with devils filled,
Should threaten to undo us,
We will not fear, for God hath willed
His truth to triumph through us.

—MARTIN LUTHER

CHAPTER FIVE

Victory for Your Family

EVERY FAMILY—especially those who have taken a stand for Christ—is under attack. I see the results of Satan's devastation everywhere—lives in conflict, marriages torn apart, and children in rebellion.

The enemy wants nothing more than to destroy the home. It is an institution designated by God as the foundation for our lives, a place of security where we nurture our children and enjoy a sense of peace.

"Please pray for my son," a woman in California writes. "He has become involved with a teen gang and I fear for his life."

A man in Michigan sent this urgent request: "Our precious daughter ran away from home last week. We haven't heard from her and fear for her safety. Please pray!"

I know firsthand how the enemy can infiltrate our lives and attempt to wrench our families apart. Barbara and I have spent many sleepless nights crying out to the Lord on behalf of our children. Thank God, He heard our prayers.

OUR LITTLE GIRL

Recently, Barbara recalled the troubling times we experienced when our daughter Becky was in her teens.

I want Barb to tell you the story in her own words:

"When Becky was born, David and I were so happy! We had prayed for a little girl and, with our son Ben, we felt our family was complete. Becky was a very good baby. She followed a routine right from the start, and it was easy for me to plan around her schedule.

"Becky was a precious child. I fussed over her and made her look like a doll. I would dress her up with bows in her hair and cute little matching outfits.

"When it was time for Becky to start school, she was so excited. Becky was always my social butterfly and loved to be with people. She also really enjoyed learning. I volunteered at school activities, so that I could be a part of all aspects of her life. We had such fun!"

THE STRUGGLE

"Becky was an excellent student, involved in cheerleading, scouting, church, and dance.

"When the opportunity came for us to move from San Diego to Charlotte to lead Inspiration Ministries, I tried to make the experience as positive as I possibly could for our children—even traveling with Becky to Charlotte early so she could try out to be a cheerleader for the coming year. She was so excited when she made the squad!

"The move proved to be difficult for our children, yet the Lord always kept His hand of protection on them. Ben went through a tough time in his life, and Becky was no exception.

"There was a period of almost a year when she struggled in her walk with the Lord. It was causing great anxiety in our home. At one point, I was so distraught with her behavior that I couldn't believe she was the same sweet, precious girl I had given birth to. I was searching for answers."

BOMBARDING HEAVEN

"Then the Lord made it clear to me that I needed to enroll Becky in a summer church camp—but she didn't want to go. She and I had gone through some difficult months and, to be honest, she didn't like me much at that point. However, I believe God had an appointment to keep with her.

"When I finally drove her to the church and put her on the bus, Becky wouldn't even kiss me goodbye. Immediately, I returned home and began bombarding Heaven with a mother's prayers. I fasted, sought God, and told the Lord, 'I'm not letting go of You until You intervene in Becky's life.'

"During that time there was a song I listened to over and over again for comfort. The verse went something like this: 'Lay it down on Mount Moriah, giving up what you love most. Giving in complete surrender that you might know God's faithfulness.'

"I totally gave Becky to the Lord during that time. I wanted God to have His way in her life—in every possible area. I spent hours praying and crying before the Throne of God. I quoted Scriptures the Lord had given me as promises for her life. I repeated them over and over again."

THE PHONE RANG

"I will never forget what happened that week. It was in the middle of the morning while I was sitting in the den, crying out to God, that the phone rang.

"'Hello,' I answered.

"'Hi, Mom. It's me, Becky. Listen Mom, I don't have much time because we only have one common phone here at camp, and the kids are all lined up to call home. I just had to tell you this. Everything is okay! I'm in love with Jesus. I love you and Dad. I'll tell you all about it just as soon as I get home. I love you Mom. Bye!'

"'Oh, Becky, I love you too, honey. I'll see you in a couple of days. Bye.'

"Well, you can imagine my reaction! I hung up the phone and shouted for joy! I cried tears of thanksgiving—and the Lord and I had a party! I was so overjoyed that I could not thank Him enough.

"Dave and I picked Becky up from camp. She literally ran and threw her arms around us and couldn't kiss us enough—right in front of the other campers! She was so full of joy I could hardly believe it.

"When she left for camp, she was depressed, rebellious,

and filled with anger. Now, this girl standing in front of me was my Becky, only better.

"We took her to dinner, and all she could do was share what the Lord had done for her that week. Her Bible was by her side, and it was underlined all over the pages."

SATAN'S DECEIT

"The lie Becky had earlier bought into was something I didn't think could ever happen in our home, which showed me how evil and deceptive the devil is. Our daughter told us she felt the things she had done were so bad that the Lord could never forgive her.

"We had raised our children in an environment of grace and mercy, yet that was the very arena in which the devil tried to defeat her! This experience taught me how much I need to ask the Lord for discernment regarding the strategies of the enemy when I pray for anyone—including those in our family.

"Today, Becky is a wife and the mother of two wonderful little boys, Samuel and Matthew. Dave and I continue to be so proud of her. She is truly a woman of God."

HOPE FOR YOUR HOUSEHOLD

The story Barbara has shared may not be nearly as troubling as the one your family is currently suffering. I know that whenever there is strife, there is also tremendous heartache. But believe me when I tell you that God loves your children even more than you do. He wants to deliver them from whatever bondage the enemy is using to enslave them.

There were days when Barbara and I wondered when—or *if*—God would give us back our children, but with persistent prayer, He responded to the cries of our heart.

Will you *totally* surrender your son, your daughter, your spouse—or even your mother or your father—to the Healer of Broken Hearts? He will mend your shattered dreams.

Keep praying. Keep believing. When Paul and Silas were miraculously delivered from prison, the guard who brought them out asked, *"'Sirs, what must I do to be saved?' They said, 'Believe in the Lord Jesus, and you will be saved, you and your household'"* (Acts 16:30-31).

God is already at work—for you and every member of your family. Don't give up or give in before you receive a breakthrough.

PRAYER CHANGES THINGS

You may ask, "If I want to change the behavior of someone I love, what approach is best—the carrot or the stick? Should I use rewards or punishment?"

Let me suggest a better alternative. Instead of trying to accomplish the task yourself, why not ask God to handle the matter? Take it to the Lord in prayer.

Here are ten specific things to pray for:

1. Pray that you will raise your family according to God's principles.

"Fathers, do not provoke your children to anger, but bring them up in the discipline and instruction of the Lord" (Ephesians 6:4).

This is also good advice for grandparents as they nurture their grandchildren.

2. Pray that you will effectively teach God's Word to your children.

"These words, which I am commanding you today, shall be on your heart. You shall teach them diligently to your sons and shall talk of them when you sit in your house and when you walk by the way and when you lie down and when you rise up" (Deuteronomy 6:6-7).

Passing on our faith to our children or grandchildren is not an event, but rather a lifestyle. We reflect our love for God in everything we do.

3. Pray that your sons and daughters will find Christ.

Paul writes to young Timothy, *"from childhood you have known the sacred writings which are able to give you the wisdom that leads to salvation through faith which is in Christ Jesus"* (2 Timothy 3:15).

The spiritual destiny of Timothy was greatly impacted by the prayers of both his mother and his grandmother (2 Timothy 1:5).

4 . Pray that your children will walk in truth.

John told the early Believers, *"I was very glad to find some of your children walking in truth, just as we have received commandment to do from the Father"* (2 John 1:4).

In the life of our family, we must love what is honest and true.

5. Pray that you will honor and respect every member of your family.

God's Word tells us, *"Do not merely look out for your own personal interests, but also for the interests of others"* (Philippians 2:4).

Strong families are built on love, trust, and consideration of one another.

6. Pray that you will speak with kindness.

"Let your speech always be with grace, as though seasoned with salt, so that you will know how you should respond to each person" (Colossians 4:6).

In my experience, kids can detect hypocrisy a mile away. Make certain your words and actions add up—especially in your household. Determine that with God's help, you will live with integrity.

7. Pray that you will be an example of love.

"Therefore be imitators of God, as beloved children; and walk in love, just as Christ also loved you and gave Himself up for us, an offering and a sacrifice to God as a fragrant aroma" (Ephesians 5:1-2).

It's what you do, not what you say that will impact your family the most.

8. Pray for a spirit of forgiveness.

"Be kind to one another, tender-hearted, forgiving

each other, just as God in Christ also has forgiven you" (Ephesians 4:32).

We serve a God of grace and mercy—so we must emulate Him if we are going to create a home that is a haven for our families and guests.

9. Pray that God will bring harmony to your home.

"Behold, how good and how pleasant it is for brothers to dwell together in unity!" (Psalm 133:1)

Ask the Lord to use you as an instrument of healing and unity in your home.

10. Pray that God will bless your family.

"I will pour out water on the thirsty land and streams on the dry ground; I will pour out My Spirit on your off-spring and My blessing on your descendants" (Isaiah 44:3).

Ask and you will receive!

YOU ARE GOD'S CHILD

I am believing with you that God will place a hedge of protection around every member of your family. If your heart is heavy because of a broken relationship or a conflict that can't seem to be resolved, allow the Holy Spirit to be your Counselor and Guide. Then place the problem at the foot of the Cross—believing by faith that Jesus will answer.

You may not know how the Lord will change the circumstances in your family, yet you can be confident that in due season, He will see you through.

MY PRAYER FOR YOU

Heavenly Father, I bring Your child and every member of their household before Your throne today. May the anointing of Your Holy Spirit be present in their home— restoring any broken relationship and healing every heartache. I pray that You will pour out Your blessing and love on Your child and their family. In Jesus' name. Amen.

GREAT IS THY FAITHFULNESS

Great is Thy faithfulness,
O God my Father,
There is no shadow of turning with Thee.
Thou changest not,
Thy compassions they fail not,
As Thou hast been Thou forever wilt be.
Great is Thy Faithfulness!
Great is Thy faithfulness!
Morning by morning new mercies I see.
All I have needed Thy hand hath provided.
Great is Thy faithfulness, Lord unto me.
—THOMAS O. CHISHOLM

Victory for Your Health

THE ADVANCES OF MEDICAL SCIENCE are mind-boggling. Yet millions remain fearful concerning their physical condition. They fret and worry:

- Will the health problems of my parents also affect me?
- Will the foods I eat cause heart disease or cancer?
- How can I be protected from the deadly viruses plaguing our world?

Often, our worst fears become reality. The doctor says, "I regret to inform you that you have breast cancer." Or, "The catheterization shows that two of your arteries are clogged. We will need to do bypass surgery."

Suddenly, your anxiety level rises like an express elevator.

"Now what?" you ask.

THE PRAYER OF FAITH

I was raised in a home where faith and belief for physical healing were not only accepted, they were expected! If there was sickness in our home, Dad would pray for us with great authority and conviction.

He believed the words written by the Apostle James, "*Is any sick among you? Let him call for the elders of the church; and let them pray over him, anointing him with oil in the name of the Lord: And the prayer of faith shall save the sick, and the Lord shall raise him up*" (James 5:14-15 KJV).

We believed that medical doctors were part of God's plan to bring healing, but we also trusted the Lord for miracles—answers that were beyond human ability.

My parents prayed, and God touched our bodies.

As I grew older, I traveled with my father to crusades and have personally witnessed blind eyes opened and deaf ears unstopped. That is why there is not the slightest doubt in my mind that God still heals today.

Now, as parents and grandparents, we pray for our family with the same fervor and faith.

IN A PANIC

"I'm worried," said Barbara, as she clutched our infant son Ben in her arms. "Feel his forehead. It's burning with fever."

Ben was our first child—and this was the first time he had shown any serious signs of illness. Naturally, we began to pray for him.

The readings on his baby thermometer kept rising— 102 degrees, 103 degrees. In a panic, we phoned our family physician for help. "Give him a bath in cool water," he counseled. "If the temperature doesn't go down, bring him straight to the emergency room."

We followed the doctor's advice, then took Ben's temperature once again. "Oh, no," Barbara exclaimed. "The reading is 104 degrees!"

STANDING ON THE WORD

Immediately, we began making plans to rush him to the hospital. There, in the family room of our San Diego home with little Ben cradled in Barbara's arms, I said, "Let's wait just a minute. I think we need to call on God one more time."

I could hear the words of the Apostle James ringing in my head.

Seated on our couch, we laid our hands on Ben's forehead, anointed him with oil, and began to call on God with great urgency: "Lord," I said, "we are standing on your Word. We are asking You to heal our son of whatever is causing this fever."

I still remember that moment with great emotion, because while we were still praying, we actually *felt* his temperature plunge. It wasn't as if his fever broke— with the sweating that usually takes place. No. One moment he was burning with fever, and the next he was perfectly normal.

We took another temperature reading and it was 98 degrees! It was truly miraculous.

"SOMETHING'S WRONG"

Let's fast-forward the calendar many years. Ben was in his early twenties, married, and living in Charlotte, North Carolina. Despite his relatively young age, he was a superintendent for a national homebuilder, overseeing the construction of rather expensive properties.

"This is Jessica," the phone call began. It was Ben's wife. "I'm at Mercy South Hospital," she continued, with an anxious tone in her voice. "We had to bring Ben to the emergency room. Something's wrong with his heart, and we're not sure what it is."

Barbara and I rushed to the hospital to learn that, for some unknown reason, Ben's heart rate had accelerated to 183 beats a minute, even while at rest, lying down, with an IV in his arm. He was plugged into monitors, and doctors were scampering in and out of the room.

I pulled one physician aside and asked, "What do you think has happened?"

"We're not sure," he replied. "We have given him medicine, but his heart rate is still elevated."

What was our response? I think you already know. We gathered as a family, anointed Ben with oil, and prayed the prayer of faith.

Nothing happened.

We continued to petition God for his healing, yet Ben's heart was still racing.

"WHY GOD? WHY?"

Two hours, now three, had gone by, and we were still

calling on the Great Physician. There was little improvement. Ben's heart rate was still over 160—a dangerous number. The medicine they had given him seemed to be having little effect.

"Why, God? *Why?*" I pleaded.

The Lord had healed Ben instantly as an infant. Now our prayers seemed to be bouncing off the ceiling.

In the emotion of the moment, here's what we failed to grasp: God was in complete control of the situation and knew exactly what He was doing.

At that time Ben had not fully committed his life to Christ. He had not truly decided whether he was going to serve the Lord with his *whole* life.

A WAKE-UP CALL

At the hospital, things took an amazing turn. The doctors never specifically diagnosed what was wrong, but within a short time, his heart rate returned to normal.

Later, he confided, "You know, Mom and Dad, in that hospital room I was frightened. I wasn't sure if I was going to live or die."

As he explained it, "I began to think about two things. First, 'If I die, where am I going?' Second, 'What has my life really accomplished? What have I done for the Lord?'"

In retrospect, I believe God gave Ben a major wake-up call. The Lord was saying "Young man, it's time to get off the fence and decide whether you're going to follow Me."

The medical emergency caused Ben to recommit his life to Christ. He made a radical decision to serve God for the rest of his days.

"YOU DON'T UNDERSTAND, DAD"

The door of my office opened one afternoon, and there stood Ben. I could tell he wanted to talk.

"What's up, son?" I asked.

"Dad," he began, "I really think God wants me to come to work with you in the ministry. I believe the Lord is calling me to be part of what He is doing here at Inspiration Ministries."

Inside, I was bursting with joy, but I hid my feelings.

"I think you need to take some time to pray and think about this," was my calm reply.

"You don't understand, Dad," he persisted. "I *have* prayed about it. And I've been waiting for three months to tell you."

"Well, I want you to go away and pray for at least another three months," I gently insisted.

"I'M RESIGNING!"

Ninety days later, Ben was back. "Dad, I waited and have done what you asked, and I feel stronger than ever that this is what God wants for my life. Is there a place for me at the ministry?"

"Of course there is," I assured him. I was excited about the thought of my son joining me in ministry.

Immediately, Ben told his boss at the construction firm that he was resigning.

"Why?" the contractor wanted to know. "Are you unhappy? Is it the money?"

Although Ben was already making a good living, his boss asked, "What will it take to get you to stay?"

Ben tried to explain, "I don't think you understand. This doesn't have anything to do with my salary or money. It concerns something I feel God wants me to do."

Ben is now ministering alongside Barbara and me as we pursue God's destiny for Inspiration Ministries and work together to impact people for Christ worldwide through media.

NOW I UNDERSTAND

Just because God miraculously healed our son as an infant did not mean He would answer in the same way at every crossroad of his life.

At the crisis point of Ben's heart condition, it would have been easy to complain, "God, where are You? Why haven't You brought healing?" After all, in both cases we had prayed the same prayer.

Now I understand. The Lord allowed that experience for His divine purpose. God works in different ways at different times in our lives.

THE KEY

"You have no idea what I am going through," a sick friend once told me.

"That's it!" I quickly interjected. "You have just found the key!"

"What are you talking about?" he replied.

"You said you are going *through* this illness. That means there are better days ahead."

The psalmist writes, *"Yea, though I walk through the valley of the shadow of death, I will fear no evil: for thou art with me; thy rod and thy staff they comfort me"* (Psalm 23:4 KJV). We don't wallow in our times of trouble—but we don't race through them either our and miss the instruction of the Lord. These valleys are God-given passageways to maturity in Christ.

As we read the writings of the Apostle Paul, we learn that he suffered from a *"thorn in the flesh." He writes to the Believers at Corinth, "...there was given me a thorn in the flesh, a messenger of Satan to torment me—to keep me from exalting myself!"* (2 Corinthians 12:7)

Theologians debate just what that "thorn" was. Personally, I believe it was some kind of physical ailment with his eyes because of what he later describes.

Paul writes, *"You know that it was because of a bodily illness that I preached the gospel to you the first time; and that which was a trial to you in my bodily condition you did not despise or loathe, but you received me as an angel of God, as Christ Jesus Himself. Where then is that sense of blessing you had? For I bear you witness that, if possible, you would have plucked out your eyes and given them to me"* (Galatians 4:13-15).

HIS GRACE IS SUFFICIENT

Whatever the malady, it's clear that the condition was

painful and humiliating. Like Job, God *permitted* Satan to afflict Paul.

He prayed three times for God to remove the thorn from him, and the Lord answered, *"My grace is sufficient for thee: for my strength is made perfect in weakness"* (2 Corinthians 12:9 KJV).

That's why the apostle could say, *"Most gladly therefore will I rather glory in my infirmities, that the power of Christ may rest upon me"* (v. 9). Then he adds, *"Therefore I take pleasure in infirmities, in reproaches, in necessities, in persecutions, in distresses for Christ's sake: for when I am weak, then am I strong"* (v. 10).

Can you believe it? Power is perfected in weakness! His grace is sufficient. Are you beginning to comprehend *why* the Lord allows you to face a physical trial?

When times of trouble seem to fall like rain—when you are buffeted by Satan and feel you have lost your ability to cope with the situation—that's when God steps in. He will give you the strength to go *through* these valleys.

GOD'S PROMISE OF HEALING

I love the words of the song, "Take your burdens to the Lord and leave them there."

Just as the Lord performed miracles as He walked the shores of Galilee and the dusty streets of Jerusalem, He has an answer for you. Some will be healed today, others tomorrow—and all who enter Heaven will be made whole for eternity.

Claim the promises of God for your healing.

Believe God will heal you.

"If the Spirit of Him who raised Jesus from the dead dwells in you, He who raised Christ Jesus from the dead will also give life to your mortal bodies through His Spirit who dwells in you" (Romans 8:11).

Believe miracles are for today.

"They shall lay hands on the sick, and they shall recover" (Mark 16:18 KJV).

Believe nothing is too difficult for the Lord.

"Behold, I am the LORD, the God of all flesh; is anything too difficult for Me?" (Jeremiah 32:27)

Believe God will remove your sickness.

"You shall serve the LORD your God, and He will bless your bread and your water; and I will remove sickness from your midst" (Exodus 23:25).

Believe the Lord can lengthen your days.

"He asked life of thee, and thou gavest it him, even length of days forever and ever" (Psalm 21:4 KJV).

Believe there is an answer for your problems.

"Why are you in despair, O my soul? And why have you become disturbed within me? Hope in God, for I shall yet praise Him, the help of my countenance and my God" (Psalm 42:11).

Believe God forgives and heals.

"*Bless the Lord, O my soul, and forget none of His benefits; Who pardons all your iniquities, Who heals all your diseases*" (Psalm 103:2-3).

Believe the Lord will make you whole.

"*I will restore you to health, and I will heal you of your wounds*" (Jeremiah 30:17).

Believe there is healing in the Word.

"*My son, give attention to my words; incline your ear to my sayings. Do not let them depart from your sight; keep them in the midst of your heart. For they are life to those who find them and health to all their body*" (Proverbs 4:20-22).

I am believing today for these Scriptures to come alive in your spirit. May they feed your faith and calm your troubled heart. Ask the Lord to heal every infirmity, and trust Him for the timing.

MY PRAYER FOR YOU

*Heavenly Father, I pray for weakness to be replaced
with strength and tears to be replaced with joy in this one's
life. Let the healing, restoring power of Your Son
quicken Your child's body, heal their wounds, and
bring a song of praise to their lips.
In Jesus' name. Amen.*

THE GREAT PHYSICIAN

The great Physician now is near,
The sympathizing Jesus;
He speaks the saddened heart to cheer,
O hear the voice of Jesus!
Sweetest note in angels' song!
Sweetest name on mortal tongue!
Sweetest carol ever sung,
Jesus, Blessed Jesus!

– WILLIAM HUNTER

CHAPTER SEVEN

Victory for
Your Finances

EVERY WEEK AT INSPIRATION MINISTRIES, we open hundreds of prayer requests from people across America—and around the world.

My heart was moved with compassion when I read a letter from a woman, who was so distressed about her finances that she was thinking about dying. She wrote, "My bills are piled high. I'm way behind on my house payment. I have a stack of bounced checks on the kitchen table, and I don't know where to turn!"

What an honor it was to pray with her that the Lord would turn her burdened heart back to the God of all comfort and provision.

Prayer is at the core of our ministry. Our ministry staff is dedicated to touching the Throne of God for those in need.

In recent months, we have seen a dramatic increase in the number of letters from individuals, who are extremely concerned about the economy—especially their own. One man wrote, "Dear David and Barbara: Please pray for me and my family. Our company recently downsized, and I was given a pink slip. I'm worried about my finances and how I will be able to provide for my wife and children."

SO MANY QUESTIONS

Ours is a troubled world where corporations collapse and pension funds vanish. Many are deeply concerned about their financial future. They wonder...

- What will happen to my 401(k)?
- Is my job secure?
- Will we have the funds to send our children to college?
- What will happen to my Social Security and Medicare benefits?
- How will I feed my family and keep a roof over our heads?

One newspaper reader commented, "I was looking for the stock market report and found the obituary page. The news was almost the same!"

A DESPERATE DAY

Barbara and I know firsthand what it's like to be without a job—with no income and wondering, "How will we make it through the week?"

It was a desperate day in the late 1970s when our bank account was zero, and our pockets were painfully empty.

At the time, Ben was just a baby. We went up to his nursery, cracked open his piggy bank, and found nearly two dollars in dimes, nickels, and pennies.

The three of us drove to a McDonald's and shared a Big Mac. I could hardly eat, worrying, "Where will our next meal come from?"

On my desk lay a stack of overdue bills, and I prayed, "Lord, how can we make our house payment? What will happen to our car?"

Believe me, we stayed on our knees, knowing God would answer—but *how?* And more important, *when?*

"CAN YOU HELP US?"

During those troubled times, I had scores of resumes circulating. Despite the urgency of our situation, there were two job offers that I declined, because in my heart I simply didn't feel that was what the Lord wanted for us. One was from a large direct marketing firm on the East Coast.

God seemed to be saying, "Be patient. I have something better for you."

Several well-known ministries heard that I was available and inquired, "Can you help us?"

I would talk with them about their needs—direct mail, program ideas, or television production. Yet, not one of those contacts resulted in a job offer.

TRYING AND FAILING

Truly believing I had a wealth of knowledge to share with large ministries, I created a one-man consulting firm and offered my services nationwide.

Whenever a ministry called, I'd rush out a proposal to

them. What I would send was designed to make it easy for them to say, "Yes!"

When I would make the follow-up call, however, my heart would sink. They were no longer interested.

This rejection became a trend. Week after week I was caught in a nerve-racking cycle of trying and failing. I was a desperate man on a mission—attempting to do it all myself.

One day, discouraged and on my knees in prayer, I clearly heard the Lord telling me, "You have done all you can. Why don't you rest in My promises and leave it in My hands?"

OUT OF THE BLUE

"Is this David Cerullo?" the person asked when I answered the phone.

"Yes it is," I replied.

The caller was from a company I had never heard of in our city. He began, "We're planning to do a prime-time television special, and we need help. Someone gave us your name and said you know something about media production and, more importantly, you have experience placing programs on stations. If that's true, we would like to talk."

"Sure," I said, trying to suppress my surprise at the call that seemed to just come out of the blue. "I'd be happy to meet with you."

"When can you be here?" the man asked.

"How about this afternoon?" I answered—trying not to sound too anxious.

"HOW MUCH WOULD YOU CHARGE?"

Three hours later I was in the office of the president of the company, and he was giving me the details for the one-hour nationwide special they envisioned.

It was a secular organization that wanted my help in navigating the waters through script writing, production, cost estimates, and media placement. They bombarded me with dozens of questions: "If we go through an ad agency, who will give us the best deal? What stations will clear the time for us?"

Finally, the president asked, "Are you interested in working up a proposal for your consulting? Do you have the time to take on this project?"

"Yes," I replied without hesitation, thinking, "If only they knew my situation!"

Then came the most essential question: "Well, how much would you charge us for your services?"

I have no idea how I arrived at the figure, but I blurted out, "I would need $3,500 to prepare a blueprint for you to follow. It will tell you all you need to know to accomplish the project."

In those days, that was a significant amount of money—and enough to meet our immediate needs.

"NO PROBLEM."

I fully expected the president to negotiate the price, but to my surprise he didn't blink. "No problem," he said. "Write up a contract outlining what we've discussed, do the work, and we'll pay you on delivery."

I'm sure they thought it would take a while for me to create the letter of agreement, so they must have been shocked when I delivered it the next day.

"I just want to confirm the scope of the project," I said, handing them the agreement to sign. Then I added, "I want to confirm that I will be paid on completion."

"That's our deal," he assured me.

This man had no idea of the depth of knowledge I had in television production and time-buying negotiations. Thank the Lord, I knew the territory like the back of my hand.

"YES! YES! YES!"

Two days later after working practically around the clock, I walked into his office with a binder choking with cost estimates, production schedules, Hollywood contacts, writers, producers, directors, and ad agencies. I even detailed how they could conserve funds by forming an in-house agency to negotiate time buying.

The company was more than pleased with the detailed plan and handed me the check for $3,500.

Praise the Lord!

Friend, do you believe God knows your situation? Do you have faith that He will give you what you need for the next step ahead? Do you really mean it when you pray, *"Give us this day our daily bread"*?

If the Almighty can provide manna for the children of Israel, just think what He can do for you!

Our dire situation did not take God by surprise. He

knew our circumstances *AND* the lesson I needed to learn—to totally rely on Him.

God answered our prayers. We had money to pay our bills that month—and even more.

Suddenly, the phone rang off the hook, and other companies were saying "Yes! Yes! Yes!" Within six months, God brought me enough work to carry us through for the next several years. The projects were a joy.

I learned to "let go and let God!"

During those days, the Lord told me, "When you are finished trying in your own strength, let Me show you what I can do." Absolutely nothing I did to secure business worked, but when I put my trust in God, He released the floodgates of His blessing!

My friend, I believe with all of my heart the Lord will do the same for you. He will give you all that is required for your next step ahead.

A VITAL TOPIC

With all the trouble in today's world—war, famine, earthquakes, hurricanes, and turmoil—you may question, "Is the Lord really interested in my personal finances?" Let me assure you, He is.

- More than 2,300 verses in the Bible concern money.
- In Matthew, Mark, and Luke, one out of every six verses deals with this topic.
- Of the 29 parables told by Christ, 16 focus on finances.

It is also an important theme of the Old Testament. Moses declares, *"But you shall remember the LORD your God, for it is He who is giving you power to make wealth, that He may confirm His covenant which He swore to your fathers, as it is this day"* (Deuteronomy 8:18).

ONLY ONE REQUEST

King Solomon was the richest man who ever lived—by today's standards he would make Bill Gates look like a pauper! Examining his life, however, proves that his passion for living was not centered on wealth.

God comes to Solomon in a dream and says to him, *"Ask what you wish me to give you."* Here is Solomon's response:

"Now, O LORD my God, You have made Your servant king in place of my father David, yet I am but a little child; I do not know how to go out or come in....So give Your servant an understanding heart to judge Your people to discern between good and evil" (1 Kings 3:7, 9).

What is God's reply? The Lord says to Solomon: *"Because you have asked this thing and have not asked for yourself long life, nor have asked riches for yourself, nor have you asked for the life of your enemies...I have done according to your words. Behold, I have given you a wise and discerning heart, so that there has been no one like you before you, nor shall one like you arise after you"* (vs. 11-12).

Then comes a surprise—a bonus—from the Lord. He declares, *"I have also given you what you have not asked, both riches and honor, so that there will not be any among the kings like you all your days"* (v. 13).

SOLOMON SAYS

Today, we are not the recipients of Solomon's wealth, but rather of his wisdom. He is the author of the book of Proverbs—a treasure-trove of everyday advice that is still relevant for our lives. Here is Solomon's counsel on money:

If you plan to eat, you'd better work!

"He who tills his land will have plenty of food, but he who follows empty pursuits will have poverty in plenty" (Proverbs 28:19). If you are not able to work, the Lord has still promised to be your provision.

You'll never succeed by sleeping!

"A little sleep, a little slumber, a little folding of the hands to rest, then your poverty will come as a robber, and your want like an armed man" (Proverbs 24:33-34).

Don't squander your savings.

"There is treasure to be desired and oil in the dwelling of the wise; but a foolish man spendeth it up" (Proverbs 21:20 KJV).

Make honesty your financial foundation.

"Wealth obtained by fraud dwindles, but the one who gathers by labor increases it" (Proverbs 13:11).

Wealth is only temporary.

"*Know well the condition of your flocks, and pay attention to your herds; for riches are not forever, nor does a crown endure to all generations*" (Proverbs 27:23-24).

Give God what belongs to Him.

"*Honor the Lord from your wealth, and from the first of all your produce; so your barns will be filled with plenty, and your vats will overflow with new wine*" (Proverbs 3:9-10).

SEVEN VITAL PRINCIPLES

The person who glibly says, "Money doesn't matter," is deluded. The Bible tells us: "*Money is the answer to everything*" (Ecclesiastes 10:19).

I firmly believe that you matter to God—and so does the way you handle your money. That's why Scripture spends time shaping our perspective on investing, wealth, and finances.

If financial strains and pressures seem overwhelming, know that He is your *Jehovah-Jirah*, which means, "God our provider." He is on your side!

Let me share seven vital principles the Lord wants you to know about His economy:

1. Your Heavenly Father desires your prosperity.

"*Beloved, I pray that in all respects you may prosper and be in good health, just as your soul prospers*" (3 John 1:2).

2. What you possess comes from the Lord.

"*Every good thing given and every perfect gift is from*

above, coming down from the Father of lights, with whom there is no variation or shifting shadow" (James 1:17).

3. The Lord is your Divine Provider.

Many *"lack, and suffer hunger; but they who seek the Lord shall not be in want of any good thing"* (Psalm 34:10). *"I have been young, and now am old; yet I have not seen the righteous forsaken, or his descendents begging bread"* (Psalm 37:25).

4. Never overlook your spiritual investments.

"Do not store up for yourselves treasures on earth, where moth and rust destroy, and where thieves break in and steal. But store up for yourselves treasures in heaven, where neither moth nor rust destroys, and where thieves do not break in or steal; for where your treasure is, there your heart will be also" (Matthew 6:19-21).

5. Your wealth carries a heavy responsibility.

"From everyone who has been given much, much will be required..." (Luke 12:48).

6. Practice God's principle of Seedtime and Harvest.

"He who sows sparingly will also reap sparingly, and he who sows bountifully will also reap bountifully" (2 Corinthians 9:6).

7. Give the Lord what is rightfully His.

"Will a man rob God? Yet you are robbing Me! But you say, 'How have we robbed You?' In tithes and offerings...

'Bring the whole tithe into the storehouse, so that there may be food in My house, and test Me now in this,' says the LORD of hosts, 'if I will not open for you the windows of heaven and pour out for you a blessing until it overflows'" (Malachi 3:8,10).

YOU'RE AN HEIR!

No matter how much wealth you accumulate here on earth, it cannot buy real estate in Heaven! In the words of an old Jewish proverb, "There are no pockets in a shroud."

Your relationship to the Lord is of far more concern than your money—or the lack of it. Life is short and eternity is long.

As a Believer, you have a spiritual bank account with assets that cannot be counted. Rejoice today that you are a child of God, who will receive an incredible inheritance.

Everything your Father owns is yours! As you are faithful to Him and His Word, what you lack He will provide.

MY PRAYER FOR YOU

*Heavenly Father, I ask that You would pour out
Your blessings and provisions upon Your child—
both spiritually and financially. Let the Seeds they Sow
in faith and obedience be an act of worship to You.
Thank You, Lord, that You will receive their offerings
and sacrifices, and then multiply them back beyond
measure. May they experience Your abundance in a
new and exciting way.
In Jesus' name. Amen.*

I'VE NEVER SEEN
THE RIGHTEOUS FORSAKEN

You may be down today,
But help is on the way.
Dark clouds may dim your skies,
But He will answer you by and by.
If you take one step, He will take two;
You'll be amazed at what God will do.
I've never seen the righteous forsaken
or His seed out begging for bread.

—ARCHIE DENNIS

CHAPTER EIGHT

Seven Steps to Overcoming Times of Trouble

THE MAN WHO CAME LOOKING FOR ME at our hotel wasn't smiling. His eyes were dark and threatening.

"Give me your passport," he demanded.

We were in Belo Horizonte, Brazil—a city of two million people located about 300 miles north of Rio de Janeiro.

I was working with my father's ministry, and on this occasion, I was coordinating the details of an overseas crusade. I was working with local pastors, arranging contracts for the arena, and handling the advertising and promotion.

The meeting was to start that night, and everything on the checklist had been completed when the secret police barged into our hotel.

"Hand over your passport right now," the officer insisted. I could see a large group of policemen standing behind him.

"And where is your father?" he angrily asked. "I need his passport also."

I took a deep breath and tried to compose myself before responding. *Nervousness* isn't quite the right word—I was far beyond that.

"JUST DO WHAT I ASK!"

Somehow, I summoned the courage to look the man straight in the eyes and said, "I refuse to give you our passports. We are American citizens and those documents are our personal property. You don't have the right to confiscate them."

"Just do what I ask," commanded the officer.

"I am not giving you our passports," I defiantly repeated. Again, he demanded to know my father's whereabouts.

"Mr. Cerullo," he continued, "we are here to inform you that you are going to be arrested and deported. We don't ever want you to return to this country." Then he added. "If your father walks onto the platform of the stadium to preach tonight, that's exactly what will happen to both of you!" Needless to say, the political climate was not favorable toward the Gospel.

He then suggested another option: "If you choose, however, to voluntarily pack your bags and go, we will allow you to leave the country without being arrested."

When I didn't give an answer, he and his fellow officers walked out of the lobby of the hotel and drove away.

AN ALTERNATE PLAN?

Immediately, I went upstairs to my father's room and told him what had just occurred. Then I offered this suggestion, "Dad, rather than leave the country, why don't you have one of the Brazilian pastors speak tonight."

After all, the major focus of his ministry has been the training of nationals. That's why he had felt called to come to Belo Horizonte.

I reminded my father, "Many times I've seen you pick some minister-in-training from the audience and say, 'Mario, you are going to preach tonight. Or, Gloria, you are going to pray for the sick.'"

It was his way of having students put into practice what they had learned in the School of Ministry—and to show the audience that all are equal in God's sight, because He is no respecter of persons.

"WHAT WILL HAPPEN?"

With that in mind, I encouraged him to choose local ministers to conduct the service.

"No," he responded, "I can't do that. Not tonight!"

"Why not?" I wanted to know. "Don't you understand the alternative? We will be arrested and thrown in jail."

"No, the meeting will go on as planned," insisted my father.

"Are you sure?" I pressed him. "We might be deported. And before that, we'll be sitting in jail for who knows how long!"

Dad calmly replied, "If I choose to take that route, I would be showing these young ministers that I'm afraid. I'd be setting an example that when adversity strikes your life, you use an excuse or you just cop out."

"No," he continued, "I'm walking onto that platform tonight, and I will preach. That's what God sent me here to do—and if the Lord chooses for us to be arrested and thrown in jail, so be it. And if we sit there for a day, a week, a month, a year, or even get deported, that's God's plan and His purpose. We are going to stay true to the mission to which God has called us."

My father was telling me two important things: (1) You need to stand in the conviction that God will be with you, and (2) He is still with you, even if the outcome isn't what you expect. Jesus is still Lord!

That was a troubling day, and much prayer was invested the rest of that afternoon. I kept looking at my watch wondering, "What will happen tonight?"

A SHOW OF FORCE

Forty thousand Brazilians jammed the indoor arena that evening. They were shoulder-to-shoulder, most of them standing.

What a sight as we drove up to the facility—there were soldiers everywhere! I don't mean a few dozen or a few hundred. The presence of armed military numbered in the *thousands!* Plus, there were armored personnel carriers and machine gun nests.

A very impressive show of force! At every entrance,

exit, and stairwell stood soldiers carrying rifles.

When I saw the scene unfolding before my eyes, I commented, "Dad, it looks as though they are expecting an invasion from another country!" My heart skipped a few more beats.

SOLDIERS ON EVERY SIDE

Slowly, we drove through lines of armed soldiers and the growing crowd trying to make their way into the crusade. The area where we were to park was inside the facility under the arena.

When we stopped and opened the doors of the vehicle, there were soldiers flanked on every side. I thought, "We're going to be arrested! This is it!"

I was shocked when not one person made a threatening move or said a word. We walked through the armed men up to the platform, and my father preached an anointed message.

It was amazing. Not a finger was lifted to turn people away or disrupt the service in any manner.

When the altar call was given at the close of the meeting, thousands came to the altar to receive Christ— including several hundred of those soldiers.

What a victory we had in Belo Horizonte!

OBEDIENCE BRINGS BLESSINGS

Why did God protect us, calm our fears, and bless our efforts? I believe that despite my concern, it was because we were faithful:

- Faithful to what God told us to do
- Faithful as a ministry team
- Faithful as servants of the Almighty

It is through obedience that blessings come. The Bible says, *"If thou shalt hearken diligently unto the voice of the LORD thy God, to observe and to do all his commandments which I command thee this day, that the LORD thy God will set thee on high above all nations of the earth: and all these blessings shall come on thee"* (Deuteronomy 28:1-2 KJV).

As I learned in Brazil, when you have the courage of conviction to make the right decisions, the Lord will stand with you. Even if the answer doesn't arrive the way you expect it, God is sovereign and the Lord of all your circumstances. How He chooses to act is His prerogative. His ways are higher than our ways.

Regardless of the sudden pressures that come, stand on your faith and trust the Lord for the outcome.

VITAL SEVEN STEPS

Anxiety is described by author Arthur Roche as "a thin stream of fear trickling through the mind. If encouraged, it cuts a channel into which all other thoughts are drained."

You may be wondering, "How can I prevent worries from dominating my thoughts and affecting my life?"

Let me recommend these seven vital steps:

1. Ask the Lord to examine your heart.

Start by allowing your Heavenly Father to shine a

bright light into your soul and mind. Pray the words of the psalmist: *"Search me, O God, and know my heart; try me and know my anxious thoughts"* (Psalm 139:23).

Measure your behavior against Ephesians 4. If your heart is honest before God, it will be reflected in your actions:

- *"Be renewed in the spirit of your mind"* (Ephesians 4:23).
- *"Speak truth each of you with his neighbor, for we are members of one another"* (v. 25).
- *"Be angry, and yet do not sin and do not let the sun go down on your anger,"* (v. 26).
- *"and do not give the devil an opportunity"* (v. 27).
- *"Let no unwholesome word proceed from your mouth"* (v. 29).
- *"Do not grieve the Holy Spirit of God"* (v. 30).
- *"Let all bitterness and wrath and anger and clamor and slander be put away from you, along with all malice"* (v. 31).
- *"Be kind to one another, tender-hearted, forgiving each other, just as God in Christ also has forgiven you"* (v. 32).

Let me encourage you to be transparent before the Lord. When you confess your faults and live in obedience, the pressure you are under begins to lift. You can breathe freely again!

2. Present your troubles to the Almighty.

Because of pride, we often hang onto our cares and concerns, thinking, "I can handle this myself."

If we try in the natural to throw our problems away, they have a tendency to come flying back at us like a boomerang, and we are right back where we started!

The Apostle Peter says, "*Humble yourselves therefore under the mighty hand of God, that he may exalt you in due time: casting all your care upon him; for he careth for you*" (1 Peter 5:6, 7 KJV).

I've met those who don't come to God's Throne because of their guilt and shame. They say, "I've failed the Lord so many times that I'm not sure He will forgive me."

Shame is part of the devil's plan to keep you in a cycle of self-condemnation. Christ offers you His cleansing, and He will remove your guilt and shame.

My friend, let me remind you that Christ understands what you are going through: "*For we do not have a high priest who cannot sympathize with our weaknesses, but One who has been tempted in all things as we are, yet without sin*" (Hebrews 4:15).

You are not disqualified or turned away because of your failures. Christ, your Advocate before the Father, invites you to receive His mercy and restoration.

Don't be timid. *Cast* your cares—discard them once and for all. Turn them over to the Lord permanently.

Paul had dozens of reasons for feeling distressed, yet while sitting in a Roman prison, he writes to the Believers at Philippi, *"Be anxious for nothing, but in everything by prayer and supplication with thanksgiving let your requests be made known to God. And the peace of God, which surpasses all comprehension, will guard your hearts and minds in Christ Jesus"* (Philippians 4:6).

3. Trust in God's love.

What is a mother's response when her toddler falls off his tricycle and scrapes a knee? She rushes over, comforts the crying child in her arms, and says, "Don't worry, it's going to be all right. Mommy loves you!"

Picture the Lord looking down on you the same way. The depth of God's love for us far surpasses our limited comprehension.

The psalmist asks, *"How long shall I take counsel in my soul, having sorrow in my heart all the day? How long will my enemy be exalted over me?...But I have trusted in Your lovingkindness; my heart shall rejoice in Your salvation"* (Psalm 13:2, 5).

Nothing can separate us from His love (Romans 8:35).

4. Fill yourself with the Word.

In the wilderness, Satan comes to Jesus and tempts Him saying, *"If you are the Son of God, command that these stones become bread"* (Matthew 4:3).

Jesus answers him with three powerful words: *"It is written."*

Quoting Deuteronomy 8:3, the Lord tells the devil, *"It is written, 'Man shall not live on bread alone, but on every word that proceeds out of the mouth of God'"* (v. 4).

Twice more (Matthew 4:7, 10), the Lord answers Satan with *"It is written."*

I cannot emphasize this too often: let your mind and heart be washed in the Word—it will be a bright and shining light to guide your steps.

Even more, become a storehouse of Scripture. In the face of every troubling time, you can remind the devil:

- Regardless of my circumstance, *"It is written!"*
- Regardless of the bad report, *"It is written!"*
- Regardless of the turmoil you try to inflict on my life, *"It is written!"*

5. Believe that God will answer.

If you need reassurance that God will hear an anguished heart, spend time in the book of Psalms. In the first few chapters, David is wringing his hands in despair.

Then something life-changing takes place. He says, *"I waited patiently for the LORD: and he inclined unto me, and heard my cry. He brought me up also out of a horrible pit, out of the miry clay, and set my feet upon a rock, and established my goings"* (Psalm 40:1 KJV).

That's why David can say with conviction, *"In the day of my trouble I shall call upon You, for You will answer me"* (Psalm 86:7).

How the Lord responds is not always in the manner we want or expect. In His sovereignty, the answers are sometimes "Yes," "No," "Not now," or perhaps even "Never."

As a parent, you don't always give your children everything they ask for or indulge their every whim.

Why? Because you are looking out for their best interest.

God is your Father. Trust Him to make the right decisions on your behalf.

By the time we reach Psalm 91, David is not only testifying about God's deliverance, he is telling others, "The same thing can happen to you!" He writes, "*He shall cover thee with his feathers, and under his wings shalt thou trust; his truth shall be thy shield and buckler*" (Psalm 91:4 KJV).

It makes no difference what life throws in your path; you are *always* covered by God's protection. Stand tall in that confidence, and don't let Satan have the satisfaction of causing you to doubt the Lord's eternal goodness.

6. *Allow the Lord to rescue you.*

Don't give up!

Just as God delivered the three Hebrew children from a fiery furnace, the Lord will rescue you.

David says, "*He sent from on high, He took me; He drew me out of many waters*" (2 Samuel 22:17).

Your troubling times are temporary—they won't last forever. The Word declares, "*After you have suffered for a little while, the God of all grace, who called you to His eternal glory in Christ, will Himself perfect, confirm, strengthen and establish you*" (1 Peter 5:10).

Be patient! Divine help is on the way. God works *all* things for our good—constantly guiding, leading, strengthening, and conforming us to Himself.

Jesus is the One you can trust to have your best interest at heart. He desires that you live a peace-filled, joy-full life.

7. Give thanks for all things!

It's easy to say, "Thank you, Lord," for the good things—a job promotion, an unexpected bonus, a healthy new grandchild, or a visit to a family reunion. But what is our response when things go wrong?

According to the Word, we must be *"Giving thanks always for all things unto God and the Father in the name of our Lord Jesus Christ"* (Ephesians 5:20 KJV).

If you want to view your problems from God's perspective, start praising Him. It will elevate you into His Presence, and you'll suddenly be looking down on your troubles rather than being buried under them.

Even learn to give God thanks in advance of His blessing. That's what the armies of Israel did when they were being invaded by the armies of Moab, Ammon, and Mount Seir. Even before the battle began, King Jehoshaphat *"appointed those who sang to the LORD and those who praised Him in holy attire, as they went out before the army and said, 'Give thanks to the LORD, for His lovingkindness is everlasting'"* (2 Chronicles 20:21).

Think of it! While they were singing and praising God, the enemy was routed!

Let your anxious moments become an altar of worship and praise. As Paul exclaims, *"But thanks be to God, who always leads us in triumph in Christ, and manifests through us the sweet aroma of the knowledge of Him in every place"* (2 Corinthians 2:14).

When you know that God has a purpose and design for your future, you can praise Him with every step you take—those that move you forward and even those that set you back. It's all part of the Master's plan to make you the fragrance of Jesus and to bring to Himself the greatest glory.

HIDDEN STRENGTH

I know it's difficult for your spirit to be serene and calm when the winds are howling, and it seems the very foundation of your life is shaking.

But with the Lord at your side, you have hidden strength—a commodity most people don't understand. Jesus says, *"My peace I give unto you: not as the world giveth give I unto you. Let not your heart be troubled, neither let it be afraid"* (John 14:27 KJV).

Don't look to your job, your family, or your own strength for your way of escape. Your rescue comes from the Lord. He is your Deliverer and Strong Tower. *"I will lift up mine eyes unto the hills, from whence cometh my help"* (Psalm 121:1 KJV).

In all these things—troubles, worries, fears, and distress—*"we are more than conquerors through him that loved us. For I am persuaded, that neither death, nor life, nor angels, nor principalities, nor powers, nor things present, nor things to come, nor height, nor depth, nor any other creature, shall be able to separate us from the love of God, which is in Christ Jesus our Lord"* (Romans 8:37-39 KJV).

There's a celebration of victory ahead!

MY PRAYER FOR YOU

Heavenly Father, in the midst of adversity,
I pray that You will enable Your child to praise
and worship You. Help them to give You thanks for all
things—even those things that they don't understand.
May they feel the presence of Your Holy Spirit covering
their life and giving peace to their soul.
In Jesus' name. Amen.

THE SOLID ROCK

When darkness veils His lovely face,
I rest on His unchanging grace;
In every high and stormy gale,
My anchor holds within the veil.
On Christ, the solid rock I stand;
All other ground is sinking sand.

—EDWARD MOTE

CHAPTER NINE

The Power of Persistent Prayer

OUR DAUGHTER BECKY was only four months into her second pregnancy when, unexpectedly, she began having contractions.

She and her husband Chip were extremely concerned—as were Barbara and I—when she was rushed to the hospital.

"I don't understand it," Becky told us. "My first baby was carried to term with absolutely no problems. What is happening?"

For some reason, the baby wanted to make an early arrival, and the doctors couldn't get the contractions to stop. But as people of faith, we knew what to do when that disturbing phone call came:

- We prayed.
- We trusted God.
- We came against the spirits of death and the work of Satan's curse.
- We bound principalities and powers that were trying to harm our daughter and this precious new life.

• We interceded on Becky's behalf.

• We spoke words of life.

Then, we literally took God at His Word when He says, *"...and having done all...stand"* (Ephesians 6:13 KJV).

I wish I had the insight to know why some prayers are answered in an instant and others are not. In Becky's case, God responded in a very short period of time. Her early contractions ended, and she was able to carry the baby to term.

Praise God! Today we have a beautiful, healthy grandson named Matthew.

A RELENTLESS SPIRIT OF PRAYER

No war has ever been won by employing a defensive strategy, and neither can the war against the enemy be won in this way. You must be on the offensive. Go after it! It's time to take back the emotional and spiritual land in your life. God tells us to *"possess the land"* (Deuteronomy 9:23).

During times of trouble, you need to take back what the world, the flesh, and the devil have stolen from you. This is not a time to sing the old Christian anthem, "Hold the fort, for I am coming." Instead, rise up and move forward!

When Christ was in the Garden of Gethsemane, spiritual warfare was raging. Luke 22:44 describes Jesus as being in agony and sweating great drops of blood.

The original word for "agony" refers to a place of contest or a battlefield—highly descriptive of true intercession.

Paul writes, *"Now I urge you, brethren, by our Lord Jesus Christ and by the love of the Spirit, to strive together with me in your prayers to God for me"* (Romans 15:30).

AN ATTITUDE OF AUTHORITY

God expects us to use our God-Given authority in troubling situations. He says to the Prophet Jeremiah, *"See, I have this day set you over the nations and over the kingdoms, to root out and to pull down, to destroy and to throw down, to build and to plant"* (Jeremiah 1:10 KJV).

According to this Scripture, interceding begins as we *"root out"* evil. With the help of the Holy Spirit, we identify the source of the problem. Remember, these roots are hidden, and we must dig deep for them.

"To pull down" suggests that we remove an object from a high position. Ephesians 6 talks about principalities and powers, rulers of darkness, and wickedness that are in the heavenly, high places.

Next, God asks us to *"throw down"* what is unnecessary—removing it quickly.

In its place, we are *"to build"* and reestablish broken lives according to God's blueprint.

Finally, we are *"to plant,"* to Sow Seed where it has the greatest capacity to grow. That's how lives are changed.

I believe the heart of God is moved on our behalf as we demonstrate selflessness in our intercession for others. James 5:16 encourages us to, *"Pray for one another, so that you may be healed."*

A BURDEN OF PRAYER

Prayer must be a cry that echoes from the inner recesses of your soul.

Don't be ashamed to release your emotions. The writer of Lamentations describes how the hearts of the people cried out to the Lord:

"O wall of the daughter of Zion, let your tears run down like a river day and night; give yourself no relief, let your eyes have no rest. Arise, cry aloud in the night, at the beginning of the night watches; pour out your heart like water, before the presence of the Lord" (Lamentations 2:18-19).

Go ahead and let the tears flow: *"The Lord is near to the brokenhearted and saves those who are crushed in spirit"* (Psalm 34:18).

Our tears are precious to God—He stores them in a vessel. The psalmist writes, *"You have taken account of my wanderings; put my tears in Your bottle"* (Psalm 56:8).

The Lord treasures those who are tenderhearted and broken in spirit toward others. Tears provide life-giving water to the spiritual Seeds we Sow. As Charles Spurgeon expressed it, "Tears are liquid prayer."

The Word declares, *"Those who sow in tears shall reap with joyful shouting. He who goes to and fro weeping, carrying his bag of seed, shall indeed come again with a shout of joy, bringing his sheaves with him"* (Psalm 126:5-6). Practice the principle of Sowing and Reaping, Seedtime and Harvest, and water your Seeds with your tears. Your barns will be full and overflowing!

POTENT PRAYER!

When our supplication is combined with God's strength, what an awesome power! We can only stand back in amazement.

The fastest link between Heaven and earth is prayer. The moment we call on God, He is waiting and ready to respond.

Don't worry about the critics and naysayers who are always with us. When you ask the Lord to intervene, all things are possible!

Today, add faith and expectancy to your prayers. In the words of the psalmist, *"My soul, wait thou only upon God; for my expectation is from him"* (Psalm 62:5 KJV).

Believe it when you say to your personal mountain, "Be thou removed!" The hand of God responds to the power of your prayer.

Oswald Chambers observed, "Jesus carries on intercession for us in heaven; the Holy Ghost carries on intercession in us on earth, and we the saints have to carry on intercession for all men."

You may have to make some tough decisions to distance yourself from people who discourage you or simply fuel your anxiety during times of trouble. Don't worry. The Lord also will send those who will lift your spirits and help you celebrate the promises of God.

MY PRAYER FOR YOU

Heavenly Father, give Your child a heart of compassion and love. As they intercede for others, pour out Your blessings on them. I pray that You will enable them to leave their cares and concerns at the feet of Jesus. In His name. Amen.

WHAT A FRIEND WE HAVE IN JESUS

What a friend we have in Jesus,
All our sins and griefs to bear!
What a privilege to carry,
Everything to God in prayer.
O what peace we often forfeit,
O what needless pain we bear,
All because we do not carry,
Everything to God in prayer.
—JOSEPH M. SCRIVEN

CHAPTER TEN

From Stress to Rest

IT'S AMAZING!

These days there is a pill for almost everything—and the big drug companies seem to have invented prescriptions for ailments we didn't even know existed a few years ago! And just in case the pills don't bring relief, there is always acupuncture, yoga, biofeedback, music therapy, or a week at the health spa!

"I've got to sit down," complained one mother. "I can feel my blood pressure rising." She had just rushed home from work in time to drive her three kids to soccer, ballet, and gymnastics classes.

She shook her head and exclaimed, "It's sure not 'Little House on the Prairie' any longer."

I believe medicine is a marvelous help when needed, but it should not become a replacement for our trust in God.

LIFE STRESSORS

We cannot put the causes of stress in one single box, because they're not the same for everyone. For example, on the job, one person may relish the challenge of a new assignment, while another may be terrified. One may be extremely productive working against a deadline, while another can barely cope under such pressure.

Let me ask you, "What is the most stressful situation you have come up against?"

A research team posed that same question and here were the top six answers:

1. The death of a spouse.
2. Going through a divorce.
3. Getting married.
4. A pregnancy.
5. Buying a house.
6. Christmas.

Whatever the cause—from being the caregiver for a child who is mentally challenged, to pressing financial worries—you will know stress when you feel it! It puts a damper on your spirit and frazzles your nerves.

Some describe their reactions to stress this way:
• "At times, I cry uncontrollably."
• "A tightness comes into the muscles of my neck and jaw."
• "I turn to comfort foods to make me feel at ease."
• "I often feel overwhelmed and confused."
• "I have increasing digestive problems and heartburn."

REAL OR IMAGINED?

Talk to enough people, and they will tell you how

extreme tension can affect Your thoughts, emotions, behavior, body functions, and physical health.

Perhaps the most dangerous reaction is that tension produces a constant rush of adrenaline that over stimulates the heart, and eventually weakens the immune system. When that occurs, we have opened the door to a variety of illnesses.

Here's the amazing part: your brain doesn't differentiate between real or imagined sources of stress. Whether you are undergoing a tax audit or watching a scary movie on television, it's all the same to your brain!

THE BATTLE FOR YOUR MIND

You may say, "David, are you telling me it's all in my mind?"

As we will see from Scripture, the answer is, "Yes." The moment stress rears its ugly head, you have a choice to make—and the battleground for making this decision is found in the mind.

Moving from stress to rest begins with a mental decision. You have two choices: you can succumb—or overcome!

The causes may be varied, but if your thoughts trigger the stress hormones, look out!

I've heard it said, "Life acts and you react."

Sadly, in our drive-thru, fast food, hurry-up world, many are headed for a crash. The tension builds like a tightly wound spring until, suddenly, it snaps.

Have you ever dealt with weeds? In a matter of days,

they can invade your flowerbeds and ruin your carefully planned garden.

Emotional and spiritual weeds are no different. They need to be ruthlessly eliminated while they are still small and before they overtake and strangle your life. That's why we need to keep our hearts pure and our minds set on Christ Jesus.

Don't dwell unnecessarily on pain or worry, allowing seeds of doubt to take root. Instead:

- Identify the source of your stress.
- Stand guard against it.
- Stay in the Word.
- Take your concerns before the Lord.

My friend, if you will apply this cleansing approach to the times of trouble in your life, the Lord will protect you from outside intrusions. He will replace your tension-filled moments with a spirit of peace that brings victory.

REPAIRING YOUR MIND

I am concerned about what is taking place in your home, at your job, with your health, and in your relationships. I don't want you to become another statistic.

I want you to know that God has a way to ease the pressure and stress you may be under today. He desires that your heart be at peace and you mind be at rest.

Just as worry divides your mind, there is something that can unite it. It's called *peace,* and it has the amazing ability to repair what stress has injured. You receive it by:

- Living under the shadow of the Almighty
  (Psalm 91:1-2).
- Making a commitment to avoid strife
  (Proverbs 20:3).
- Knowing the Prince of Peace
  (Isaiah 9:6; Luke 24:36).

You see, *"God is not the author of confusion, but of peace"* (1 Corinthians 14:33 KJV).

There's a crucial battle being fought—and I'm not referring to the war against terrorism or godless nations. This conflict is being waged between your ears for the ultimate control of your thoughts. Satan realizes that if he can invade your mind, every other part of your body will crumble. That's why Paul says, *"We are destroying speculations and every lofty thing raised up against the knowledge of God, and we are taking every thought captive to the obedience of Christ"* (2 Corinthians 10:5).

You need to stay focused, not allowing your mind to wander. Let me encourage you to spend time reading what Paul writes to the church at Philippi. In Chapter 4 of his epistle, he proclaims, *"The peace of God, which surpasses all comprehension, will guard your hearts and your minds in Christ Jesus"* (v. 7).

PRICELESS ADVICE

Paul makes reducing the pressures of life easy for us, even telling us what to think about:

"Finally, brethren, whatsoever things are true, whatso-

ever things are honest, whatsoever things are just, whatsoever things are pure, whatsoever things are lovely, whatsoever things are of good report; if there be any virtue, and if there be any praise, think on these things" (Philippians 4:8 KJV).

That's priceless advice. If our nation put just that one Scripture into practice, thousands of psychologists would be looking for another occupation.

In the next verse, Paul takes us one further step. He tells us how to turn our thinking into action: "Those things, which ye have both learned, and received, and heard, and seen in me, do."

Then, if we move from belief to behavior, the Apostle tells us, "and the God of peace shall be with you" (v. 9).

I hope you are beginning to see the Biblical alternative to stress and worry. When your mind is overflowing with good thoughts—God thoughts—there is no room for anxiety! "Thou wilt keep him in perfect peace, whose mind is stayed on thee, because he trusteth in thee" (Isaiah 26:3 KJV).

Don't delay another day: "Set your mind on the things above, not on the things that are on earth" (Colossians 3:2).

THE CLEFT OF THE ROCK

In Mississippi, a psychiatrist posted a small sign in his waiting room that read, "Y'all calm?"

However you may say it, that's what so many people need—a life that is tranquil.

Billy Graham eloquently described "peace" when he gave this illustration in one of his messages. He said, "The storm was raging. The sea was beating against the rocks in huge, dashing waves. The lightning was flashing, the thunder was roaring, the wind was blowing; but the little bird was sound asleep in the crevice of the rock, its head tucked serenely under its wings. That is peace: to be able to sleep in the storm!"

If you are still searching for a way to escape the pressures of life, let me recommend a Person rather than a place. His name is Jesus, and He says *"Come to Me, all who are weary and heavy-laden, and I will give you rest. Take My yoke upon you and learn from Me, for I am gentle and humble in heart, and you will find rest for your souls. For My yoke is easy and My burden is light"* (Matthew 11:28-30).

A NEW PERSPECTIVE

Mistakenly, some people think, "If I could just get a promotion and increase my salary, I know my stress would be gone." Or, "If we could only move to Florida, life would be so much easier."

Let me assure you that your income and environment have little to do with easing your tension and finding peace. You need a new perspective—a fresh view of your present circumstances.

I recently heard of a Chinese pastor, who was given a three-year prison sentence for declaring his faith. While incarcerated, he began sharing his testimony, telling his fellow inmates about the forgiveness of Jesus and His unconditional love. Many were won to Christ. After two years, the government offered him an early release but to their surprise, he refused.

Why did this man refuse the chance to be free? Why was he content to call a guarded cell his home? Because God had given him a mission—and he knew his work in prison wasn't completed.

The Lord can redeem any hardship for His glory if we will surrender to His desire for our circumstances. An eternal perspective sees beyond the bars of a jail cell to our future homecoming with Christ.

THE DIVINE SOURCES

All of Heaven is involved in helping to turn your stress into rest. There are three sources of peace:

1. The Father—"the peace of God" (Philippians 4:7)
2. The Son—"peace be with you" (John 20:26)
3. The Holy Spirit—"love, joy, peace" (Galatians 5:22)

Do you remember how heartbroken the disciples are when Jesus is about to return to Heaven? The One they have grown to love is about to leave them, and Peter says, *"Lord, why can I not follow You right now?"* (John 13:37)

No one, not even Peter, likes uncertainty. The followers of Christ are unsure and worried how the Lord's work will continue without Him.

Jesus consoles them with these comforting words: *"Let not your heart be troubled: ye believe in God, believe also in me. In my Father's house are many mansions: if it were not so, I would have told you. I go to prepare a place for you. And if I go and prepare a place for you, I will come again, and receive you unto myself; that where I am, there ye may be also"* (John 14:1-3 KJV).

Before returning to His Father, the Lord says, *"Peace I leave with you, my peace I give unto you: not as the world giveth give I unto you"* (v. 27).

Yes, Jesus is leaving, but He promises to return.

"COME UNTO ME"

I have great news! You don't have to wait for Christ's second coming to know peace. I trust you have experienced the saving work of Christ, and have asked Him to forgive your sin. He purchased your peace at Calvary. *"But he was wounded for our transgressions, he was bruised for our iniquities: the chastisement of our peace was upon him; and with his stripes we are healed"* (Isaiah 53:5 KJV).

When you have accepted Christ, your heart can be filled with the Word. You can develop an intimacy with the Father that will calm your fears and bring you to a place of perfect peace.

Today, say goodbye to the stranglehold of stress by…

Setting aside a time every day to be alone with God.

Quiet yourself before the Lord: *"Be still, and know that I am God"* (Psalm 46:10 KJV).

Placing a "No Trespassing" sign on your heart and mind.

Shut the door on negative thoughts: *"Watch over your heart with all diligence, for from it flow the springs of life"* (Proverbs 4:23).

Choosing how you will spend your time.

Set a schedule that will develop spiritual growth: *"So teach us to number our days, That we may present to You a heart of wisdom"* (Psalm 90:12).

Knowing your limits.

Don't overextend yourself and take on more than you can handle: *"For He Himself knows our frame; He is mindful that we are but dust"* (Psalm 103:14).

Giving thanks to the Lord for His peace.

"Let the peace of Christ rule in your hearts, to which indeed you were called in one body; and be thankful" (Colossians 3:15).

It's time to make a choice:

- Will you worry or will you worship?
- Will you know stress or know the Savior?
- Will your life be filled with pressure or be filled with peace?

Let the winds blow; let the storms rage; the Lord is still saying to you, *"Peace, be still."*

MY PRAYER FOR YOU

Heavenly Father, today, I come before You on Your child's behalf. I pray that You will remove any harmful and distracting thoughts from their mind. Fill them with Your love. May they know rest beyond measure and the peace that only Your Son, our Prince of Peace, can bring.
In His name. Amen.

HE HIDETH MY SOUL

He hideth my soul in the cleft of the rock,
That shadows a dry, thirsty land;
He hideth my life in the depths of His love,
And covers me there with His hand.

—FANNY CROSBY

CHAPTER ELEVEN

It's a Promise!

I SMILED when I heard about a three-year-old girl who was acting up in church—right in the middle of the pastor's message. Her embarrassed mother grabbed the little girl in her arms and was marching down the middle aisle toward the back door when the child screamed out, "Somebody help me! She's going to kill me!"

Outside, the girl was heard pleading with her mom, "I promise I'll be good. Really, I promise!"

We all go through life making pledges:

- "I need you to sign this promissory note," said the car dealer as he handed me the keys to our new car.
- "Do you vow to love, honor, and obey?" asked the minister as the bride and groom stood before the altar.
- Every time you use an ATM machine or sign a credit card slip, you are in essence saying, "I promise!"

When presented with a document that you must personally guarantee, you have three choices:

- You can reject it: "I think I'll pass."
- You can be skeptical: "I'm not sure about this."
- You can accept it: "I agree to the terms."

Friend, you need to know that God has also made promises to you—and they are permanently recorded in His Word.

You may worry, "I've read the wonderful things the Lord says He will do for me, but I'm not sure I deserve them." Well, don't feel alone:

- The Hebrew children in the desert didn't deserve water from a rock—yet God gave it to them because of His Covenant with His people.
- Jonah didn't deserve to be rescued from the belly of the great fish—but the Lord needed a preacher in Nineveh.
- The 5,000 who showed up to hear Jesus preach on a hillside near the Sea of Galilee, didn't deserve to be fed—but the Lord demonstrated His compassion and care by multiplying the loaves and fishes.

When God makes a promise, He keeps it. This is what gives us hope for the future and comfort for today.

Paul says to Timothy, *"If we are faithless, He remains faithful for He cannot deny Himself"* (2 Timothy 2:13).

In the Amplified Bible, this verse reads, *"If we are faithless [do not believe and are untrue to Him], He remains true (faithful to His Word and His righteous character), for He cannot deny Himself."*

What a blessed assurance! Everything we have from the Father is a gift—salvation, peace, provision, and our future home in Heaven. No, we don't deserve these benefits, yet the love of God is so great that we are called His sons and daughters.

Although you cannot earn salvation, you can intentionally develop a heart of trust and a spirit of worship toward the Father, Who hears your every cry.

"SHAKE IT OFF!"

Let me share with you a story about a farmer who owned an old mule. One day the animal fell into a rather deep well that was located on his property. A few minutes later, the man heard the frightened mule loudly braying.

The farmer, after mulling over the situation, had sympathy for the animal, but decided that neither the old mule, nor the well, was worth the trouble of saving. He then called his neighbors together and told them what had happened. "Will you help me haul some dirt to bury my old mule? I think we ought to put him out of his misery."

When the first shovel-full of dirt was thrown down the well, the mule went hysterical! Then, as the dirt continued to rain down on him he had a brilliant idea. The mule said to himself, "Every time dirt lands on my back, I'm going to shake it off and step up!"

For what seemed an eternity, he stuck with his plan. "Shake it off and step up! Shake it off and step up!"

It didn't matter how plentiful the dirt or how painful

the blows, that old mule gritted his teeth and toughed it out—shaking it off and stepping up.

Eventually the animal—dirty, battered, and exhausted—stepped right out of that well!

What was meant to bury him wound up *blessing* him. He escaped because of the way he handled adversity.

TRUST AND OBEY

The children of Israel were moving toward the Promised Land, yet their story was one of complaints and anguish as they labored through the desert for 40 long years. They learned the hard way that God's promises are conditional.

The Bible says, *"Commit thy way unto the LORD; trust also in him; and he shall bring it to pass"* (Psalm 37:5 KJV). His promises aren't for everyone—only for those who faithfully accept, and obey, God's Covenant with them.

When your faith is combined with obedience, you will experience the Presence, Provision, and Power of God like never before. And if you have failed, run quickly into the forgiving arms of Jesus to experience His mercy anew. Hallelujah!

THE DREAMER

I love talking with teens—they have a special place in our ministry. Thanks to our Partners, who have chosen to impact lives for Christ with us, we are producing programs that do just that. Together, we are winning people to Christ.

Let me tell you about a young man in the Bible, who was only 17 years old when God made a promise to him in a dream. His name was Joseph—a son of Jacob in the land of Canaan.

What the Lord revealed was unusual. God gave him a promise that he would become a leader—and even his brothers would bow down to him.

First, his jealous brothers staged his fictitious death and put him into a deep pit. Then they sold Joseph into slavery, and he wound up in Egypt, where he rose to a place of authority—a governor—under Pharaoh. You can read the story in Genesis 37-47.

A great famine swept over Canaan, causing Jacob to send his sons (Joseph's brothers) into Egypt to buy corn. In the process, they had to come to the governor's palace and bow before him. At that moment, God's promise to Joseph was fulfilled!

What a shock when the day finally came that Joseph revealed himself as the brother they had sold into slavery years earlier—and what a glorious celebration when he was reunited with his father! (Genesis 46:29).

Later, the brothers again fell on their faces before Joseph, asking for his forgiveness. And here is his response: *"But as for you, ye thought evil against me; but God meant it unto good"* (Genesis 50:20 KJV). *The Bible says, "...he comforted them, and spake kindly unto them"* (Genesis 50:21).

I don't know what trials you are walking through today; you may be languishing "in the pit" like

Joseph—with your life destroyed by forces you can't seem to control.

Take heart! What God promises, He completes—and even your times of trouble may be meant for your good.

LISTEN, WATCH, AND WALK

Most Christians never hear the audible voice of God, yet they can know when He is speaking, and providing directions that can change life's circumstances. Let me encourage you to listen to His words, watch for His vision, and walk through His open doors.

Noah is an old man when the Lord speaks to him saying, *"I establish my covenant with you, and with your seed after you"* (Genesis 9:8-9 KJV).

God makes a promise to Noah that if he builds the ark, Noah, his family, and two of every living creature would be saved from the flood to begin a new civilization on the earth.

Noah listens and responds in faith, and the Lord keeps His vow.

WHAT HE PROMISES, HE PERFORMS!

What does the Almighty promise Abraham? He says, *"I will make of thee a great nation, and I will bless thee, and make thy name great; and thou shalt be a blessing: And I will bless them that bless thee, and curse him that curseth thee: and in thee shall all families of the earth be blessed"* (Genesis 12:2-3).

Years later, when both Abraham and his wife Sarah

were growing old, God announces, "You are going to have a son." Abraham is about 100 years old and thinks Sarah's womb is barren, *"yet, with respect to the promise of God, he did not waver in unbelief but grew strong in faith, giving glory to God, and being fully assured that what God had promised, He was able also to perform"* (Romans 4:20-21).

Abraham *believes,* and God provides a son just as He declared He would.

THE HOUSE OF DAVID

Later, God makes a Covenant with David when He declares, *"And thine house and thy kingdom shall be established for ever before thee: thy throne shall be established forever"* (2 Samuel 7:16 KJV).

When you read the "begat" genealogy in the first chapter of Matthew, you discover that this is the lineage that leads to the birth of Jesus. The angel that appears to Joseph, proclaims, *"Thou son of David, fear not to take unto thee Mary thy wife: for that which is conceived in her is of the Holy Ghost"* (Matthew 1:20 KJV).

Let me take this moment to ask, "What has God promised you? What has He told you would take place in your future?"

Despite David's years of obscurity as a shepherd, and even when his own father overlooks him, God sees the heart of a king.

GIFTS FROM YOUR FATHER

You may ask, "Why would God talk with *me?* I'm

not important. Surely He doesn't care what I am going through."

My friend, let me assure you that the Lord doesn't look at status, gender, seniority, or skin color. We are all equal in His sight. All who call on Him *"are given unto us exceeding great and precious promises: that by these ye might be partakers of the divine nature"* (2 Peter 1:4 KJV).

Here's what your Father pledges to you:

God promises abundance.

"Blessed is the man that trusteth in the LORD, and whose hope the LORD is. For he shall be as a tree planted by the waters, that spreadeth out her roots by the river, and shall not fear when heat cometh, but its leaf shall be green; and shall not be careful in the year of drought, neither shall cease from yielding fruit" (Jeremiah 17:7-8 KJV).

God promises protection.

"But thou, O LORD, art a shield for me; my glory, and the lifter up of mine head" (Psalm 3:3 KJV).

God promises power.

"Do not fear, for I am with you; do not anxiously look about you, for I am your God. I will strengthen you, surely I will help you, surely I will uphold you with My righteous right hand" (Isaiah 41:10).

God promises faithfulness.

"For the LORD will not abandon His people on account of His great name, because the LORD has been pleased to make you a people for Himself" (1 Samuel 12:22).

"*I will never leave thee nor forsake thee*" (Hebrews 13:5 KJV).

JOY IS COMING!

At this very moment, you may be at a low point in your walk with God. I want to reassure you once again that Barbara and I are praying for you. We love you and believe the Lord wants to raise you up and set you free.

Let me remind you, "*Many are the afflictions of the righteous: but the Lord delivereth him out of them all*" (Psalm 34:19 KJV)—not "some," but "*ALL*"!

I am claiming God's promises for you, so that your fears will subside and your tears will end. The Bible tells us, "*Weeping may endure for a night, but joy cometh in the morning*" (Psalm 30:5 KJV). What a glorious hope!

"I WILL!"

God has written hundreds of promises for you. Now it's your turn! As a result of reading this book, I pray you will be able to say:

- I will turn my times of trouble over to the Lord.
- I will use God's Word to fight my fear.
- I will practice the Father's principle of Seedtime and Harvest.
- I will believe God for healing and health.
- I will give thanks for all things.
- I will defeat Satan through the name of Jesus.

- I will pray and intercede for those who need a touch from God.
- I will listen to the Lord when He says "Peace, be still!"
- I will, by faith, stand in victory!

YOU CAN REJOICE!

If the Apostle Peter were writing the last page of this book, he would tell you: *"In this you greatly rejoice, even though now for a little while, if necessary, you have been distressed by various trials, so that the proof of your faith, being more precious than gold which is perishable, even though tested by fire, may be found to result in praise and glory and honor at the revelation of Jesus Christ"* (1 Peter 1:6-7).

What a wonderful assurance! You may be walking though distressing and troubled times, yet you are able to lift your hands to Heaven and praise the Lord!

You can declare, *"Though the fig tree should not blossom, and there be no fruit on the vines, though the yield of the olive should fail, and the fields produce no food, though the flock should be cut off from the fold and there be no cattle in the stalls, yet I will rejoice in LORD, I will rejoice in the God of my salvation. The LORD God is my strength, and He has made my feet like hinds' feet, and makes me walk on my high places"* (Habakkuk 3:17-19). Amen!

Beloved, the Lord wants to establish and strengthen you in every area of your life, regardless of what your circumstances may look like.

There's something great ahead! *"Blessed is a man who perseveres under trial; for once he has been approved, he will receive the crown of life which the Lord has promised to those who love Him"* (James 1:12).

And as the Apostle Paul tells us, *"We are afflicted in every way, but not crushed; perplexed, but not despairing; persecuted, but not forsaken; struck down, but not destroyed"* (2 Corinthians 4:8-9).

Thank God, your times of trouble can bring you closer to the Lord: *"Who will separate us from the love of Christ? Will tribulation, or distress, or persecution, or famine, or nakedness, or peril, or sword?...For I am convinced that neither death, nor life, nor angels, nor principalities, nor things present, nor things to come, nor powers, nor height, nor depth, nor any other created thing, will be able to separate us from the love of God, which is in Christ Jesus our Lord"* (Romans 8:35, 38-39).

That's worth shouting about!

MY PRAYER FOR YOU

Heavenly Father, we praise You for Your mighty power, protection, and deliverance. May You give Your child a double portion of Your abundance and blessing. Today— and always—may Your child continue to embrace Your answers in their times of trouble.
In Jesus' name. Amen.

'TIS SO SWEET TO TRUST IN JESUS

'Tis so sweet to trust in Jesus,
Just to take Him at His word,
Just to rest upon His promise,
Just to know "Thus saith the Lord."
Jesus, Jesus, how I trust Him!
How I've proved Him o'er and o'er!
Jesus, Jesus, precious Jesus!
O for grace to trust Him more!
—LOUISA M.R. STEAD

ABOUT THE AUTHOR

DAVID CERULLO graduated from Oral Roberts University with a degree in Business Administration and Management.

After college, David joined his father to serve at Morris Cerullo World Evangelism and gradually assumed most responsibilities for the day-to-day operations of the ministry. He was ordained for ministry in 1974.

Because of his vision to impact people for Christ worldwide through media, David combined his strong business skills with his passion for ministry to assume the leadership of a fledgling Christian cable television network in 1990.

With God's help and guidance, David established Inspiration Ministries, an international media ministry that reaches out to more than a billion Souls worldwide with the Gospel of Jesus Christ.

He is a member of the National Cable Television Association, the Cable and Telecommunications Association for Marketing, the National Association of Television Program Executives, and has served on the Board of Directors for the National Religious Broadcasters Association.

His extensive experience in cable network management includes operations, program development, writing, producing, directing, syndication, marketing, advertising, public relations, affiliate relations, sales, sponsorship, business affairs, and finance.

David and his wife, Barbara, have been married for more than 38 years and have two adult children and five grandchildren. David and Barbara host a popular daily international television program, "Inspiration Today!"

Visit them at **inspiration.org** for a current program schedule, a ministry update, or to request prayer.

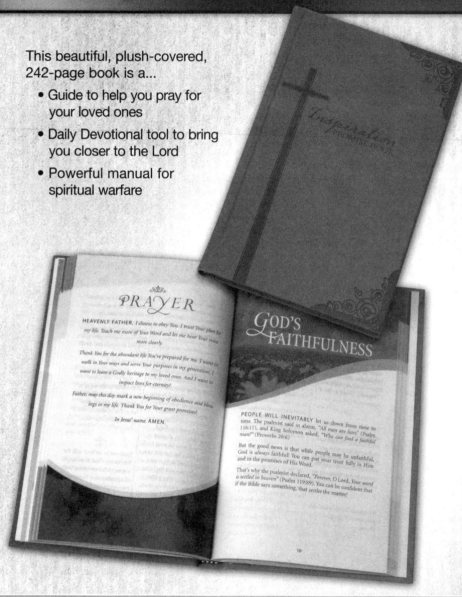

Inspiration
PRAYER JOURNAL

This lovely journal is the perfect place for you to record your prayer requests and the Specific Assignments you've given your Seeds ... write what you hear God speaking to you through His Word and in prayer ... and commemorate the Harvests He releases into your life as you live in His unending cycle of Sowing and Reaping!

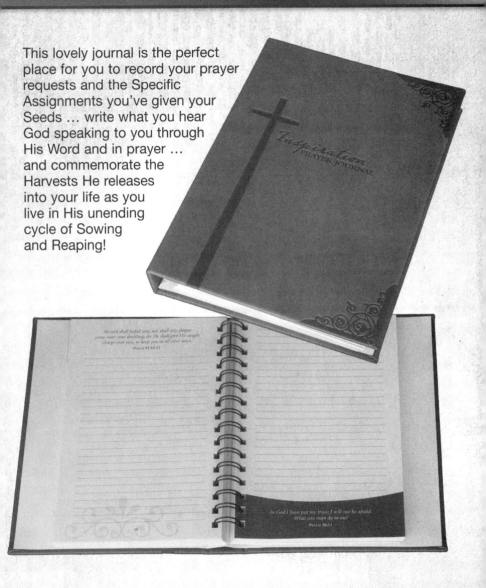

click on "Ministry Gift Offers" and receive your copy today!

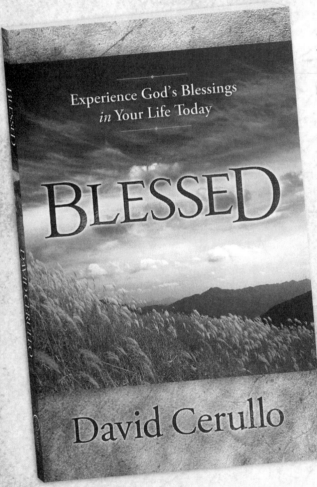

Do You Need a MIRACLE From God?

God is a God of MIRACLES!

Do you need God's supernatural intervention today in your...

- BODY, SOUL, OR SPIRIT?
- FINANCES, HOME, OR JOB?
- Relationships with loved ones?

This life-changing ministry resource will help you experience the miracle you need from Him!

"How to Receive Your Miracle tells me how to look forward to God's promises for complete healing in my life. This book has been an eye opener for me to the keys of living!" — KAREN

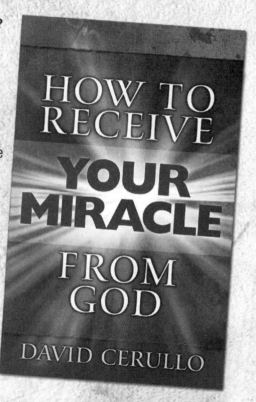

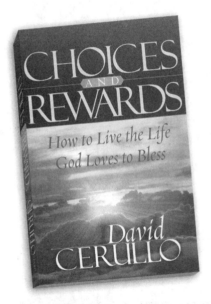

God Answers Prayer!

"If two of you agree on earth concerning anything that they ask, it will be done for them by My Father in Heaven."
— MATTHEW 18:19

"Thanks so much for your prayers for my husband Michael, who had been diagnosed with cancer. Michael went back for a check-up, and the doctor said his cancer is GONE! Praise the Lord!" — HELEN

"Your prayers and those of our friends have brought Divine healing to my mom's thyroid disease! She's returned to her former health!" — JAMES

"Thank you for having one of your prayer ministers call and pray with me today. The call came at just the right time, and it made me feel like someone really cares. Again, thank you for the call just to pray with me." — GLORIA

Our prayer ministers welcome the opportunity to agree together with you in prayer and believe God to step into the circumstances of your life with His supernatural power!

In the U.S., call 803-578-1800
7 days a week, 24 hours a day.

In the U.K., call 0845 683 0584
Monday – Friday, 09:30 – 21:30.

Or email your prayer request to Prayer@inspiration.org.

Partner Services number & hours:
803-578-1899
9 a.m. - 5 p.m.

INSPIRATION
Blessed to Be a Blessing

You'll love the daily devotionals, testimonies, and personal messages from David and Barbara Cerullo.

"Your monthly devotional magazine helps us get through the day. Our family has much adversity coming at us to steal our faith, but the devotional helps us keep trusting in God." — BILL & SUSAN

**Visit inspiration.org or call 866-324-5001
to Sow a Seed for Souls and receive a year's
subscription to this monthly ministry resource.**

"BATTLE FOR YOUR LIFE" VICTORY PACK
Will Give You the Tools You Need to Triumph Over the Enemy!

This powerful array of spiritual resources includes:

- ***Battle for Your Life.*** This timely manual will equip you to pull down enemy strongholds so you can discover God's destiny for your life!

- **Three video DVDs** of a teaching series on spiritual warfare. You'll want to watch the DVDs with your family, small group, or Sunday school class.

- **The audio CDs** of messages are a wonderful resource to listen to in your car, helping you put on the *"full armor of God"* each day!

- **A bookmark** to remind you of key Biblical principles for gaining victory over Satan. Keep it in your Bible or in your copy of the ***Battle for Your Life*** book!

Ready *for* BATTLE?

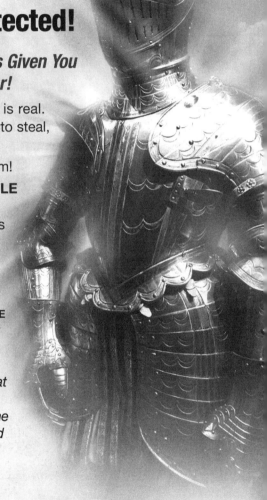

Don't Be Unprotected!

Use the Weapons God Has Given You to Win This Spiritual War!

The war is real. The enemy is real. His power is real. His agenda to steal, kill, and destroy is real.

You don't need to be a victim!

The resources in the **"BATTLE FOR YOUR LIFE" VICTORY PACK** will place in your hands the vital keys you need for victorious spiritual warfare in your life.

"I have read your book BATTLE FOR YOUR LIFE, and I see now where Satan has almost destroyed me and my family. But I'm fighting back now that I realize a real spiritual evil is assaulting my children and me and my job. Thanks, and God bless you!" — HUGH

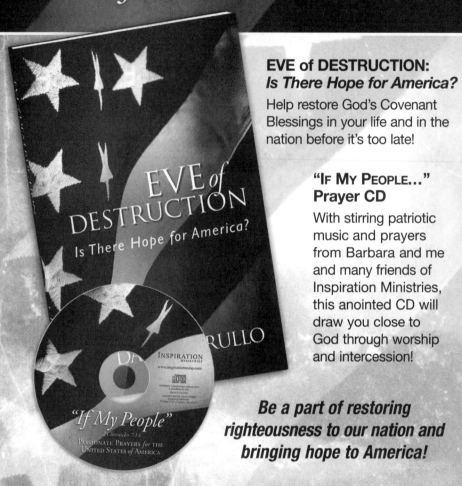